The Real Face of
Faceb**o**k
in India

The Real Face of Facebook in India

How Social Media
have Become a
Propaganda Weapon
and Disseminator of
Disinformation and
Falsehood

CYRIL SAM AND
PARANJOY GUHA THAKURTA

PARANJOY

First published in India in 2019 by:
Paranjoy Guha Thakurta
paranjoy@gmail.com

Index by Vandana Bhagra
Typeset by Ram Das Lal, NCR Delhi
Cover design: PealiDezine

Publishing facilitation: AuthorsUpFront

To all exposing and studying the politics and the effects of internet-based communication technologies on democracies.

Contents

Foreword

Dangers of Learning at the WhatsApp University

Manoeuvring messaging on Facebook is the Bharatiya Janata Party's strategy to drive the political discourse in India

By Ravish Kumar,
Senior Executive Editor, NDTV India

Whenever I get flooded with abusive and threatening calls on my mobile phone, I know my number has been shared on Facebook (FB). Typically, a member or a supporter of the Bharatiya Janata Party puts up a post on Facebook providing my number and then says: "Please don't call up Ravish Kumar." This has become "code language" for them. Soon thereafter, the phone calls start coming in. As I am writing this note on 14 April 2019, I learn that my mobile phone number together with the numbers of a few other journalists were again shared on Facebook and the post was being made viral in Aligarh (in Uttar Pradesh). The persons who have put up these posts are also sharing communally-charged content on the social media platform, thereby contributing to an escalation of aggression along religious lines. These posts – with their hidden and not-so-hidden signs – are not just destroying the soul of religion but "religion" in political democracy in the country as well. Facebook has connected me with many people. But it has also become a legally-safe instrument for people to spread rumours and hatred.

Recently, my Facebook account was shut down for a while. I was told that I had shared screenshots of messages I had received on WhatsApp (WA) from individuals whose phone numbers were visible. These messages had been sent by persons who had been abusing me and threatening me. I was told that disclosing phone numbers was against Facebook's policies. I accepted the discipline imposed on me and removed their numbers from the screenshots. I did what was told to me. But has Facebook removed the pages of those who have shared my phone number as well as the numbers of other journalists? The answer is "no." Even today these pages are up and accessible to all. They are still being made to go viral.

Facebook and WhatsApp have changed society considerably. When it started, Facebook connected people. It became the voice of the voiceless, unknown individuals. It provided space for their views. Gradually, Facebook was hijacked by the most-powerful political party together with the high and mighty in India.

The comments section on my page is filled with threats that have been meted out to me, and rumours that have been spread about me. It appears as if Facebook wants to finish this country's healthy tradition of free expression and become a tool for brainwashing people. Its character has transformed. At a local level, the social media platform has become a part of the techniques used for political management. This includes making complaints to close down pages of rivals and opponents. Facebook is no longer a social media network – it has become a political network. It is today a platform for the country's ruling party that has huge resources to spend on disseminating its propaganda. Smaller parties are thus at a big disadvantage. It has made political rivalry in a democracy one-sided. Those who run Facebook pages for the smaller parties are being threatened with their lives. This has posed challenges for local law-enforcing authorities.

After the Congress party raised the slogan "chowkidar chor hain" – meaning the "guard is a thief" – to level allegations against Prime Minister Narendra Modi in the Rafale fighter aircraft deal, in retaliation, the BJP called on its ministers and supporters to prefix the word "chowkidar" before their names on social media handles. Questions are today being raised as to whether those who are running Facebook pages for the BJP should prefix "chowkidar" before their names or "nagarik" (citizen). Facebook has become an integral part of India's ruling party's strategy to control and dominate the political discourse.

On 30 March, writing in *The Washington Post*, Facebook's founder Mark Zuckerberg suggested a more active role for governments to regulate and control the content that is placed on the internet. The same person who had earlier wanted governments to stay away from internet regulation now stressed the need for governments to improve and update rules and regulations governing the internet to protect freedom of expression. But this is a clear instance of Facebook seeking to cleverly transfer its responsbilities as governments are themselves the biggest enemies of free expression. It is completely unrealistic to expect governments to regulate social media platforms. This is just tall talk. Facebook has to devise its own structures and systems of self-regulation.

There are innumerable pages put up by political parties, politicians and their supporters on Facebook. When it cannot regulate these pages, why is it suggesting that the government do this? India's policing system and law-enforcing authorities are ill-equipped and have been completely helpless in checking the spread of rumours and hate speech on WhatsApp and Facebook. Cops in this country cannot counter the automated "intelligence" systems of Facebook and its sister social media platforms. They do not understand artificial intelligence and complex algorithms.

Controlling content on Facebook and WhatsApp will be possible only if a government sets up a regulatory body that can impose its authority on Facebook. Can such a body be bigger than Facebook? How should such a regulatory authority be created? Who should head it? How should it operate? These are all big questions to which there are no clear answers. At this juncture in India, I don't think such a regulatory authority will be able to work, leave alone be effective.

From time to time, Facebook releases transparency reports to indicate the number of hateful posts that they have removed. It is very likely that Facebook has been successful in removing some such content, but I believe that it is impossible to remove all such posts given the extent of its reach across villages and small towns spread across the length and the breadth of the country. It is difficult, if not impossible, to remove content posted in different languages and dialects. For instance, Facebook's transparency reports do not tell us anything about the number of posts in Bengali, Marathi or other Indian languages that were removed. These do not indicate the shutting-down of pages run by administrators in smaller cities and towns. Is Facebook equipped to intervene and shut down a hateful and malicious post, say, in Maithili or Bhojpuri? Very often such information is not posted directly or in a straightforward manner but follows a circuitous, roundabout route.

The impact of Facebook and WhatsApp on society is being studied and researched across the world. Books are being written on the subject. In India, however, research on the impact of social media platforms subject has lagged behind. In this country where there are large disparities in the spread of education and knowledge, there is a real and present danger that a post on Facebook will be perceived as a page from a history book. You can write anything about Jawaharlal Nehru, the first Prime Minister of India. People who read what has been posted will believe it to be true. Large sections of the youth in India have not had an opportunity to receive quality education from good teachers.

Given the poor quality of educational infrastructure in the country, many young students consider Facebook as a source of knowledge. For some of them, Facebook and WhatsApp are nothing short of a university. Whatever information is received fills up spaces in their brains. The BJP has taken advantage of the fact that it is the ruling party and has gained considerable presence in the social media. It has a firm grip over the worlds of many users of Facebook and WhatsApp.

I am happy that Paranjoy Guha Thakurta and Cyril Sam have written this book for Hindi readers. Many of such readers are far removed from the politics of "big data" and the conversations surrounding big data that are taking place around the world. This book will serve as a valuable resource for those readers who are keen on understanding the current and future dangers of WhatsApp and Facebook.

Within Facebook, there are debates and discussions that are raging. The organisation's founder, Mark Zuckerberg, was summoned by United States (US) lawmakers and questioned. Facebook is under tremendous pressure to change its ways. However, given current circumstances, what will those persons do whose brains have already been washed by WhatsApp, the ones who spread rumours and hateful content on social media platforms? Who is responsible? Can Facebook and WhatsApp absolve themselves of all responsibility? What are the responsibilities of individual users? It is crystal clear that we need to be aware of our own roles, even as we evaluate the roles of WhatsApp and Facebook and venture into the offices of the IT (information technology) cells of the ruling party in India and those of the high and mighty in the land. It has become crucial and essential for all of us to understand and appreciate the conversations around Facebook and raise questions about its activities.

(Translated from the original article in Hindi by Manish Purohit and Jayshree Guha Thakurta)

Preface

Trapped in a Toxic Echo Chamber

Does Mark Zuckerberg fancy Augustus Caesar as a role model?

By Apoorvanand,
Professor of Hindi, University of Delhi

Openness, transparency, togetherness, new communities, open networks: these were some of the promises with which Facebook came into our lives. Very soon, we found that this was actually a trap. New communities meant new echo chambers, openness and transparency meant more demands on us to bare ourselves even as eyes are fixed to measure each part of us, evaluating them as items worth a certain amount of money. We can be seen but the eyes watching us are invisible.

Nearly 15 years after Facebook opened itself up for everyone above 13 years of age, realisation has dawned that it is one huge set-up. The company's technologies are changing patterns of individual behaviour, and not always towards noble ends.

A conversation with a friend led me to introspect about the way Facebook has been changing us. She received a call from an acquaintance, a writer and a poet, who complained about her not liking a Facebook post that had been made by the acquanintance. "I am not your 'friend'," my friend candidly remarked.

After some time, the two met again and the acquaintance repeated her complaint. It was then that my friend realised that her acquaintance was expecting a "friend" request from her. It had, after all, become a matter of one's position in a hierarchy. So, you invite or cajole people into sending you a "friend" request and then delude yourself into believing that you were the one sought after.

It is this human vulnerability, a mixture of desires to be liked, to be sought after, to be befriended and be seen, that has helped Facebook grow into a kind of supra-nation, a nation in which people feel that they are autonomous beings who make their own rules. Wrote Evans Osnos in *The New Yorker* magazine in September 2018.

> If Facebook were a country, it would have the largest population on earth. More than 2.2 billion people, about a third of humanity, log in at least once a month. That user base has no precedent in the history of American enterprise. Fourteen years after it was founded, in Zuckerberg's dorm room, Facebook has as many adherents as Christianity.

This article by Osnos needs to be read to understand the mind that is behind the new empire in which we enrol ourselves as willing subjects, ever ready to part with all the information about ourselves that we are asked to provide, for which Facebook gets paid by companies and organisations that advertise. Without our knowledge we are chopped and dissected into little bits of data that are then sold.

Osnos tells us that Zuckerberg sees Augustus Caesar as his ideal figure. He explains:

> You have all these good and bad and complex figures. I think Augustus is one of the most fascinating (among them). Basically, through a really harsh approach, he established two hundred years of world peace.

The writer in *The New Yorker* was unimpressed as he knows that Augustus Caesar, born 63 years before Jesus Christ, had staked his claim to power at the age of 18 and turned Rome from a republic into an empire by conquering Egypt, northern Spain and large parts of central Europe. He also eliminated his political opponents, banished his daughter for promiscuity and was suspected of arranging the execution of his grandson.

This idea of peace should normally not be frightening for all of us. But the person who espouses it is a man all heads of states confabulate with, one who is presented as an icon of success to our children and the youth. The atrocities that Augustus committed were, in the eyes of Mark Zuckerberg, a legitimate price for a 200 year-long peace. It is a trade off, in his opinion. He, in fact, has named his daughter after Augustus.

Dominance and disruption are his mantras. The "religion of growth" is what the company believes in. It talks about increasing connectivity as if it was involved in some humanistic endeavour, breaking boundaries of nations and making people "friends." But, as Osnos explains, connectivity is a proxy or a substitute for growth. Zuckerberg and his team members feel that there should not be any impediment in this path of growth. Once they argued that American law enforcement agencies should not come in the way of this growth by asking Facebook to reveal its sources of funding of political advertisements. This, in their view, would hamper innovation.

Facebook thus sought to claim that it was above the law as it was performing a most necessary and sacred function, namely, promoting innovation for the progress of humanity. Zuckerberg has displayed a careless and a cavalier approach towards privacy and once even claimed that it was not a social norm. Researchers who have used data from Facebook without permission of the original content providers have had to express regret later. Even as the ethicality of such use of content has been discussed and debated, those on Facebook were horrified when they learnt that they had been used as guinea pigs, displayed as exhibits or bits of data without their prior knowledge or consent.

Facebook is where it is because of human frailties like self-obsession that have helped it cajole – or even force people – to give it their time and attention. Thus, on the face of things, Facebook hardly appears dangerous. Its users believe that their actions are almost voluntary. But we know that what actually takes place is far more complex. Through clever manipulation of emotions, it becomes almost impossible for individuals to understand what is being done to them and realise how they are being enslaved.

Facebook is doing social engineering on a scale never witnessed before in the history of humankind. Those at the helm of totalitarian states might even become faithful and diligent students of the organisation. The digital monopoly has not only turned all its users into discrete data but has also monetised the data along the way. All of us on the social media have been commodified. In other words, we have been alienated from ourselves and deceived into believing we are actually creating a larger, unifying self for each one of us.

Facebook is dangerous because it lulls you into numbness and then mutilates you. Psychologists the world over and political leaders have started realising the threat that Facebook holds for humanity and also for the sovereignty of nation-states. Read the following sentences to fathom the level of threat it poses to economies and to nations:

> Today's big tech companies have too much power – too much power over our economy, our society, and our democracy. They've bulldozed competition, used our private information for profit, and tilted the playing field against everyone else. And in the process, they have hurt small businesses and stifled innovation.
>
> I want a government that makes sure everybody – even the biggest and most powerful companies in America – plays by the rules. And I want to make sure that the next generation of great American tech companies can flourish. To do that, we need to stop this generation of big tech companies from throwing around their political power to shape the rules in their favor and throwing around their economic power to snuff out or buy up every potential competitor.
>
> That's why my administration will make big, structural changes to the tech sector to promote more competition – including breaking up Amazon, Facebook, and Google.

This is Elizabeth Warren, the aspirant from the Democratic Party running for the post of President of the US. She pledges to use anti-trust laws in her country to break up these giant companies in the interest of fair competition and more than that, to uphold the freedom of the individual who is being manipulated and sold to multiple buyers by these companies without her knowledge. For us it is unimaginable that a politician should be talking about breaking up a monopoly and eroding the hegemony of a corporate giant, that too in a country where communism remains a dirty word.

Before her, it was Tim Wu who thought that it was high time Facebook was broken up. Wu, who is known for his use of the term "net neutrality," argues in his book *The Curse of Bigness: Antitrust in the New Gilded Age*, that anti-trust laws be enforced against Google, Facebook, Amazon, and other huge tech companies that are a threat to democracy as they get bigger and bigger.

Democracies work best when they are not direct, not immediate. They work through mediation and deliberation. Deliberation means informed deliberation. But Facebook creates an illusion of direct democracy in which everyone can participate without any mediator. The Arab Spring, the brief uprising in Israel, the Yellow Vest movement in France and the India Against Corruption campaign in India were among such movements led by Facebook when people felt that they had become leaders. These movements did not last long.

A false sense of urgency and immediacy is created by platforms like Facebook. The digital giant can conspire to manipulate and subvert democracies. The scandal surrounding Cambridge Analytica demonstrated this aspect of the social media platform very clearly. A former employee of Cambridge Analytica admitted that the firm had used harvested data from a far greater number of users than the previously-assessed 87 million. On 17 April 2018, *The Guardian* wrote and editorial that if data is the new oil then Facebook has one of the biggest reservoirs of the new black gold. And it collaborates with agencies that want to tap it for commercial or political ends.

Zuckerberg's attitude towards peace and his careless treatment of those who deny the holocaust against Jews by describing it as just another opinion, shows his moral underpinnings and those of Facebook. His is an amoral vision, a vision where maximising profit is the ultimate aim even if it leads to the destruction of humanity in people. *The Guardian* rightly noted:

> Facebook has realised this – and that the public has become aware of its threat. The company rebranded its philosophy: it wants now to bring the world 'closer together' because in acquiring 2 billion users it has fostered divisions. The social media site is exploited by conspiracy theorists, white supremacists, hyperpartisan news sites, eastern European troll farms and Russian-backed divisive advertising. These seek to manufacture and retail a point of view by manipulating voters' fears – and their dreams.

A warning is then sounded:

> The conceit of data mining firms – and the politicians who use them – is that they could win elections by moulding electorates based on new forms of identity and new value systems. This process is accelerated by the echo chamber of social media, which allows citizens to close themselves off from wider debate and become infatuated with their own

truths. There is room for interesting ideas and alternative narratives based on facts. Diversity is the sign of a healthy ecosystem. But democracy will suffer if tech giants can exercise near monopoly power over data, with hardly any accountability about how this power is used. It needs all citizens to listen to each other, so collective decisions are considered decisions...

Whenever there is an offer of a product in any form that says it is for free, we must be skeptical. In capitalism nothing comes free. The way Facebook is trying to wriggle out of the scandals it is currently embroiled in, provides a telling testimony to this simple thumbrule.

One has to look at pictures of the smiling and laughing Zuckerberg jogging on the streets of Berlin surrounded by bodyguards and then read about how the corporate group that this high-profile CEO heads incurred huge expenditures on his security and that of his family. As *Business Insider* pointed out, despite drawing a salary of $1, Zuckerberg's "pay" more than doubled from US$9.1 million (around ₹58.6 crore) in 2017 to $22.6 million (₹157.2 crore) in 2018, mainly on account of higher security costs. An additional $13 million (₹90.4 crore) was spent on his travel.

This is indeed a farcical situation. This money doesn't fall from the air. It is the billions of users of Facebook who are being cut to pieces and sold bit by bit to different advertisers to maintain and expand this gigantic empire.

This book by Cyril Sam and Paranjoy Guha Thakurta demonstrates in a succinct manner how Facebook is distorting democracy in India. They show that Facebook and its companion platforms, WhatsApp and Instagram, are promoting the interests of the country's ruling dispensation and augmenting its right-wing majoritarian agenda. The authors write that the noise created on these social media platforms drowns the voices of sanity and elaborates on how these digital platforms are misused to spread hatred and violence against the weak and against minorities in India and in different parts of the world. Its role in the pogrom against the Rohingyas in Myanmar has been noted by international agencies.

It is necessary for us to listen to the authors and put ourselves on a state of alert. Otherwise, we are bound to lose ourselves completely while relishing an illusion of freedom.

Introduction

How Social Media Platforms have Become Propaganda Weapons

By Prabir Purkayastha,
Editor, NewsClick and President, Free Software Movement of India

This book brings out how social media today is a propaganda weapon in the hands of the Bharatiya Janata Party for spreading its message of hatred and disenfranchising certain sections of the people. It gives us a wealth of details about the kind of support that Facebook provided Narendra Modi and the apparatus of the BJP even before the 2014 elections; the close ties it had with key people in the BJP–NaMo team; and about a revolving door between this team and that of Facebook. If anybody thinks Facebook and other digital platforms are there for all of us, and it is just that the BJP or the Right uses them better, this book should correct such a perception. No, the platforms know which side their bread is buttered, and the authors show this in meticulous detail.

There are two questions we need to pay attention to. Why

Introduction

is Facebook – here only a shorthand for Facebook and other digital platforms – far more allied to the Right? This is what we see in countries like the US, India and now, Brazil. The second question is the danger such monopoly power poses to our democracy and its institutions. New technologies pose new problems, and what we are dealing with here is the old problem of how to prevent bad news (and views) driving out the good. Even if the bad is, quite often, fake, and a violation of our laws against hate speech.

Why are digital platforms so closely aligned with the Right? Silicon Valley tycoons see themselves as modern messiahs, claiming that they and their technology will build a modern and a more inclusive society. Why then do their technologies help in propagating hate and fake news?

The answer is obviously money – the old adage that those who pay the piper call the tune. Facebook and similar platforms are clearly in the business for money, and what would be considered by any society to be obscene amounts of money. It is money that drives their business model. The movements for social change do not have money. They substitute money with people – marches, mobilisation of volunteers, door-to-door campaigning – in short, struggles, big or small. In this digital age, money can be used to amplify the voice of the rich through digital platforms.

These platforms not only multiply the message, but also do what is called target advertising. They also know which sections of people are susceptible to what message, and can micro-target different sections of people with different messages: different strokes for different folks.

This is the familiar advertising model of selling goods

and services. Google and Facebook, which today control 70 per cent of the internet traffic on the planet, have acquired their massive market power through micro-targeting. While newspapers or TV channels know some broad demographies of those who read or watch their programmes, these are very broad and diffused demographies. The digital platforms know where you live, what exactly you read, what your interests are, your age, your sex, your sexual orientation and so on. They also know your caste, your religion and other identifiers that are all important in dicing up users into small slices of demographies – people who could then be receptive to a certain kind of messaging. And these demographies are not static ones; they depend on what you are selling. If you are selling books, the seller is interested in a certain kind of demography – sex, age, income, language, etc. In politics, the demographies could be quite different. Given that our data lies in computer databases of digital platforms such as Google and Facebook, it is easy to extract the kind of demographies required for selling a particular kind of product.

Selling of commodities may not have direct impact on our democracy; selling candidates, parties and ideologies do. In a democracy, we believe that we are independent citizens with very specific views. We do not think of ourselves as parts of demographies that can be influenced by targeted advertisements. But if people can be convinced to buy products based on advertising – and the advertising industry is a big business for this reason – why should we perceive politics to be different? This is what the digital media platforms have discovered. Political advertising *is* big business; parties and candidates can be sold the same way any other goods or services are sold. Find out what the buyer's interests are, and target advertising specifically for her or his interest. That it works is not surprising. After all, digital platforms like Google and Facebook are among the world's biggest monopolies today, precisely because this advertising model works.

This brings us to another issue: the power of money and the influence it wields through advertising on digital platforms. It is money power, plain and simple, that has driven the enormous growth of political campaigning on social media. In India, political parties were not brought under the limit imposed on candidates' expenditure, unless specifically spent on a candidate. This is one loophole through which the BJP has been operating. The second is the infamous election bonds that Finance Minister Arun Jaitley has introduced, by which any funding of parties by any company, either Indian or foreign, to any extent is completely legal. Even a weak-kneed Election Commission of India, which has failed to rein the egregious violation of rules by the ruling party in these elections, has made its unhappiness known in the election bonds case. A number of groups, including the Communist Part of India (Marxist) are petitioners in the Supreme Court in this case. If money power is a danger to democracy, this money power is an even bigger multiplier in the elections today due to these digital platforms. Digital platforms, with their technology and micro-targeting, multiply this power manifold, and thereby the danger to our elections in particular and democracy in general.

The last point to note is about fake news and hate campaigns. Again, these problems are not new. When newspapers became big, one of the reasons for their rise was the discovery of advertising and the money it could bring. Many of the major advertising campaigns were essentially fraudulent – selling snake oil and magical remedies for every ailment. It is this advertising of fraudulent claims that brought about the first regulations in this field – what could or could not be claimed about products. While hate speech is permitted in the US, it is banned in most countries. Germany, for example, regulates hate speech more strongly than India does.

The additional problem we now have is the more potent brew of hate speech coupled with fake news. And unlike in traditional mass media, this happens in closed groups, particularly on WhatsApp, a part of Facebook's empire. How do we ensure that hate speech is filtered out from such closed groups and fake news is controlled, particularly as we cannot see it?

I will park the larger problem of monitoring such news, as there are various mechanisms that could be used to store such messages and track down and prosecute the purveyors of fake and hate news. For now, I will restrict myself to pointing out the stake that Facebook has in such platforms not being curbed. For Facebook, virality is money. The more people see, the more potential users they have, and the more they can sell to political parties and businesses. Facebook may pay lip service to controlling fake news on its platform, but really, it is only making noises to soothe our ruffled feelings. In reality, it will fight tooth and nail any meaningful changes on its platform to curb fake news.

If we see virality as its business model, we understand why Facebook took so long to implement a simple feature on WhatsApp – so that people are not automatically added to a group without their consent. Facebook made no effort to implement this feature, called opt in with consent, and instead offered that people could opt out of such groups. This meant repeated misuse of the facility of adding people to groups, including abusive and trolling groups in which phone numbers of the targets were repeatedly added. Finally, after a directive from the Ministry of Electronics and Information Technology, this feature is now supposed to be active.

This book describes, thoroughly, how the Empire of Facebook operates; and the enormous influence it now wields over our social and political spaces. For those who believed in the utopia of a free and liberated world of social media, in which the power of propagating views would be taken away from media monopolies and restored to the people, we now have the dystopian world of Facebook and Google. Or George Orwell's *1984* meeting Aldous Huxley's *Brave New World*, the new world of digital platform monopolies.

About the book

Is Facebook in India truly independent of political influence? Not really. The world's largest social media conglomerate, that includes WhatsApp and Instagram, has in the past, and continues to at present, extend direct and indirect support to the Prime Minister of India, Narendra Modi. This support started before he assumed the position he has been holding in the world's largest democracy since May 2014. Facebook has expectedly also promoted the interests of the ruling right-wing, Hindu nationalist political party Modi heads, namely, the Bharatiya Janata Party. The neutrality of the media platform is in serious doubt during the country's 17th general elections, the outcome of which will be known on 23 May 2019.

Facebook and its platforms are under unprecedented attack across the globe. The leadership of this digital multinational corporation has been accused of a host of questionable practices in different countries and also in India. The manner in which a gunman used Facebook to live-stream the slaughter of dozens of innocent people in Christchurch, New Zealand, on 14 March 2019, attracted widespread condemnation. The

Facebook group is arguably going through its biggest-ever crisis after it was set up in the United States of America 15 years ago. It has since become the largest private organisation of its kind in the history of humankind with an estimated 2.3 billion users across the world, including over 240 million in India – the largest in any country.

There are an estimated 500 million users of the internet among India's current population of around 1.35 billion – the Telecom Regulatory Authority of India estimated the total number of SIMs (subscriber identity modules) in the country at one billion. Of the estimated 750 million mobile phones in India at the end of 2018, there were approximately 400 million smartphones that were internet enabled, against less than 160 million in 2014. The total number of users of WhatsApp in the country is said to be around 300 million – up from less than half the number at the end of 2016. While these numbers are "guess-estimates" of sorts, what cannot be denied is that the widespread and regular use of social media platforms, in particular WhatsApp, is not confined any longer to metropolitan cities or even small towns and semi-urban areas; it is being used all over rural India, even in small villages located in remote parts of the country. For many, WhatsApp is the first (and preferred) channel of communication and transmission of information of all kinds. As many as one out of three voters in India is reportedly using the platform.

Even as allegations against the monopoly for allowing its platforms to be misused have intensified globally and calls have been made to break it up, we present here an investigation into Facebook's activities in India. This report has been based on interviews (quite a few of them off-the-record) with more than 50 individuals that were conducted over a period of six months starting June 2018. We have added to the narrative information that is available in the public domain. The *NewsClick* web portal published five long reports written by us in November 2018. We have embellished what we had written earlier with additional reportage and placed this in the context of the charged atmosphere prevailing at the time of the elections to India's lower house of Parliament or the Lok Sabha in April–May 2019.

While the international digital giant claims it provides agnostic platforms for all to use, there is evidence – some of it circumstantial – to indicate that senior employees of Facebook in India have worked – and continue to work – very closely with the country's ruling party, the BJP and Narendra Modi for around nine years. Their uncomfortably close proximity to the powers-that-be in the country raises an important question. With Facebook's impartiality being questioned, to what extent will the digital media be able to influence political preferences and electoral outcomes?

Those opposed to the incumbent regime in New Delhi are seeking to counter the BJP's propaganda using the same social media platforms. How successful will Modi's opponents be in replicating his remarkable success in using digital technology to reap political gains?

The answers to these questions may never be fully known. Still, concerns have been raised – and continue to be raised– about the misuse of WhatsApp and Facebook from various quarters before different authorities, including the Election Commission of India. Facebook claims it is working with a number of government and non-government organisations to curb misuse and abuse of its platforms. However, it seems highly unlikely that this will happen in any significant manner.

In this book divided into 19 short chapters, we critically examine how Facebook and its companion platforms – notably WhatsApp – have been complicit in promoting the interests of India's ruling regime and its right-wing majoritarian social and political agenda. We examine allegations relating to the social media platforms spreading disinformation and hate speech that have led to mob lynching in different parts of the country. We also point out how critics of the Modi regime have felt marginalised by the social media platform and its associates. We then report how Facebook arrived at the dominant position it currently holds in India with more than a little help from friends and supporters of Prime Minister Modi.

Thereafter, we outline the role played by key individuals with close links to the BJP and Modi and how social media was used in propagating his party's agenda in the recent past. Subsequently, we look at the questionable activities of Cambridge Analytica in India and allegations of a possible conflict of interest pertaining to a senior employee of Facebook in India and his partner. While outlining the crises confronting one of the world's biggest internet conglomerates set up in February 2004, we reproduce a detailed questionnaire that we sent to the representatives of Facebook along with the social media platform's predictable (and somewhat fuzzy) responses to the 64 pointed questions we asked.

Across the world, criticism of Facebook intensified in the aftermath of the publication on 14 November of a 5,000-word investigation by *The New York Times* alleging a host of questionable practices by the digital giant. The company's share prices came down and particular investors called for the resignation of Mark Zuckerberg, the 34-year-old founder and chief executive officer of Facebook and his 49-year-old deputy, chief operating officer Sheryl Sandberg. While the two have sought to refute certain specific allegations levelled against them, their leadership abilities and integrity are being questioned like never before. While contextualising Facebook's international activities, our book focuses on what has happened – and is happening – in India as we complete this manuscript.

Cyril Sam and Paranjoy Guha Thakurta
New Delhi/Gurgaon
April 2019

1

WhatsApp's Weaponisation

On 22 September 2018, speaking at a public rally for social media volunteers of the Bharatiya Janata Party (BJP) in Kota, Rajasthan, party president Amit Shah remarked: "We are capable of delivering any message we want to the public, whether sweet or sour, true or fake."

To place his remarks in context, Shah first said that before the assembly elections took place in Uttar Pradesh, India's most populous province, in February–March 2017, the BJP had put together two huge groups of its supporters on WhatsApp – comprising a stupendous total of 3.2 million users. Every day at 8 am, messages would be sent to group members for them to "know the truth" about "false" information that had been published about the BJP in various publications and websites. One "smart" volunteer had put out a fabricated post claiming that Akhilesh Yadav, the then Chief Minister of Uttar Pradesh (belonging to the Samajwadi Party which is opposed to the BJP) had slapped his father Mulayam Singh Yadav. The message went viral and reached Shah.

1

The BJP president then said that this should not have been done. Nevertheless, a *mahaul* or an environment had been created. As members in the audience smirked, Shah almost-lovingly chided them: "This is something worth doing, but don't do it! Do you understand what I am saying?"

He added: "We can do this because we have 32 lakh people in our WhatsApp groups. That is how we were able to make this go viral."

The exact text of Shah's speech in Hindi is available on many media websites. The numbers he cited are truly staggering. During a recent visit to India, the global head of WhatsApp, Chris Daniels, claimed in an interview with *The Economic Times (ET)* that while the "end-to-end encrypted" platform "enables" over 200 million individuals in the country: "People sometimes find it surprising that over 90 per cent of the messages sent on WhatsApp are between two people and the majority of groups have less than ten people."

Amit Shah and the BJP's supporters, sympathisers and volunteers have evidently been far more successful than most others across the globe in using this social media platform, that is, if Daniels' figures are to be believed. There is no doubt that the BJP has been running the world's biggest – and arguably most influential – online political campaign. The party runs a parallel news and information ecosystem on Facebook, WhatsApp and Instagram (IG) steeped in hate speech, extreme speech and Islamophobia. At a time when Facebook, the largest social media platform and digital monopoly of its kind on the planet (which also owns WhatsApp and Instagram) has come under growing global scrutiny and strident criticism over its claims of neutrality and the misuse of its data by

Cambridge Analytica and others, its operations in India are being increasingly questioned, and rightly so.

While there have been allegations that supporters of Narendra Modi have frequently spread disinformation on online platforms, sometimes with the help of content marketing and technology companies, legitimate news media organisations and journalists critical of the ruling regime are complaining that they have been deliberately marginalised and, at times, even "censored" by Facebook. Here are a few instances.

On 10 August 2018, *The Caravan* was not allowed to boost an article on Facebook which was critical of the BJP president. The magazine had claimed that Shah had "misrepresented" his assets and liabilities in his affidavit filed before the Election Commission of India. The publication wanted to boost this particular article on its website on Facebook. However, approval came 11 days later by which time the story had lost quite a bit of potential for traction as the news cycle had surged ahead.

This is what Vinod K Jose, the magazine's executive editor stated in an email communication to us: "It was very strange for us at *The Caravan* to see Facebook not boosting our exclusive report of 10 August on Amit Shah hiding his loan liabilities from his electoral affidavit, as *The Caravan* has a verified account with Facebook and both organisations have partnered each other in the past in hosting public events."

Jose added that his publication's digital marketing team waited for days after initiating the review process, but got no reply from Facebook. "This made us more suspicious and we assigned a reporter to look into what was going on... (He) contacted the India head for communications at Facebook via email and although there was no reply, the block to the boost was removed 11 days after the story was published, which in the case of a hard-hitting news story makes no sense."

The Caravan received a reply from Facebook on 21 August which read: "We've reviewed your ad(vertisement) again and have determined (that) it complies with our policies. Your ad is now approved. Your ad is now active and will start delivering soon. You can track your results in Facebook Ads Manager."

Jose wonders that if Facebook found nothing wrong on 21 August, why did it block the boost for eleven days. *The Caravan* reporter Tushar Dhara even escalated his communication to Facebook's headquarters in the United States. His questions went unanswered for ten days. "Facebook has to decide how it wants to go down in Indian history," Jose remarked sarcastically. "As a channel (that believes in) free flow of information and (being a) supporter of democracy or as a gatekeeper of information and blocker of democracy…. Companies should not have two different standards for two different democracies."

In February 2019, *Huffpost India* reported that Facebook had claimed that 7,500 people had been tasked with reviewing objectionable content and this number could be augmented during the election period.

Within days of *The Caravan* article not being boosted by Facebook, there were complaints from other journalists that they were being "locked out" of their Facebook accounts for inexplicable reasons. The common factor among all these journalists was that they were writing against the ruling party and the Modi government. They included Rifat Jawaid of *Janata Ka Reporter*, Prema Negi and Ajay Prakash of *Janjwar*

4

and several journalists with *Caravan Daily* (as distinct from *The Caravan*) and *Bolta Hindustan*.

Jawaid, a former journalist with the British Broadcasting Corporation, was shut out on 27 September. He told the Kolkata-based *The Telegraph* newspaper that the Facebook page of *Janata Ka Reporter* had been blocked in 2017 after the website broke news about the controversy relating to the Rafale fighter aircraft deal. The page was restored after he complained on social media. On 27 September, "...minutes after I posted something on the Ayodhya verdict (by the Supreme Court on the building of a Ram temple at the site where the Babri mosque was demolished in December 1992), my account was disabled," Jawaid told Pheroze L Vincent of *The Telegraph*, adding: "It was restored in a day after I wrote to the nodal officer."

Portals like *Caravan Daily* and *Janjwar* that get most of their readers on Facebook were also impacted. On 1 October, five reports published in *Caravan Daily*, including one on activist Gautam Navlakha being released from house arrest on orders of the Delhi High Court was marked as "spam" by Facebook. "When we woke up on 4 October, we found both our personal accounts blocked," Negi and Prakash said, adding that they were asked for proof of their identification more than once to access their disabled accounts.

Five employees of *Bolta Hindustan* too found their Facebook accounts blocked. Vincent asked Facebook India's communications head Amrit Ahuja to respond. Forty-eight hours were sought but no response came, *The Telegraph* journalist wrote in his article published on 8 October.

A source in *NDTV India* (speaking to one of the writers

of this article on condition of anonymity) said he and his colleagues found it rather puzzling why the traction on Facebook that was received by Ravish Kumar's popular television show, "Prime Time," would inexplicably drop on particular nights when a programme that was especially critical of the government would be broadcast. One such programme on the rising prices of petroleum products had contrasted the government's response with what Modi had said when he was Chief Minister of Gujarat.

Said this source: "We were surprised when the numbers of views and shares on our Facebook page, after going up in an expected manner, suddenly stagnated. We are not sure if this was done deliberately but it was certainly out of the ordinary. We had an internal debate as to whether we should lodge a formal complaint with Facebook. We eventually decided against it because we were not sure we would be able to establish any hanky-panky."

Facebook likes to claim that it is a politically agnostic website, but it talks little about its association with particular political parties. In an emailed statement to us on its work with political parties in India, the organisation's spokesperson stated: "Facebook's policy team is focused on helping a variety of people – educators, our community, NGOs (non-government organisations) and governments – understand our policies, programmes and products to help create positive and meaningful experiences for the people who use our services. We are globally invested in critical areas of internet governance and policy development – safety, small business growth, internet access, and giving people a voice. This team works with all political parties, and we work with all of them who reach out to us for training."

Between 2012 and 2019, supporters of the BJP have spread innumerable instances of highly-problematic content on Facebook-owned platforms to promote Modi as a "saviour" or "messiah" of India's Hindus and to suppress any criticism of him. Such content has created communal tension between Hindus and Muslims and led to incidents of mob lynching in different parts of India. Over the twelve-month period till October 2018, at least 30 individuals have been lynched by mobs – quite a few of these incidents took place after messages were spread on WhatsApp accusing them of killing cows, stealing cattle, kidnapping children or for having a relationship with a person of a different religious faith.

An analysis of government data by *IndiaSpend*, a data journalism website, suggested a 28 per cent rise in incidents of communal violence in the country between 2014 and 2017. More than half these incidents took place in states where the BJP is in power, Uttar Pradesh, Bihar and Jharkhand. The website compiled information on 33 persons killed in 69 incidents of mob violence between January 2017 and July 2018.

Much of this problem is related to the way the laws of the land are administered, or not. But can this be completely delinked from the facilities that social media platforms like Facebook and WhatsApp provide that eases disseminating of information, including disinformation or fake news? These are some of the questions we need to address.

2

Government's Helplessness

In recent months, Facebook's chief executive officer Mark Zuckerberg has been asked by representatives of at least five committees constituted by the governments of Argentina, Australia, Canada, Ireland and the United Kingdom (UK), to personally appear and depose before an "international grand committee" on disinformation and fake news. In a number of countries of Europe, the US, the UK and Singapore, Facebook's representatives have been subject to intense scrutiny and sharp criticism by lawmakers. They have been directed to become more responsible, accountable and act stringently against those misusing or abusing their platforms.

The government of India has time and again criticized Facebook for the spread of disinformation. However, the government's representatives have, by and large, demanded that Facebook fix the problems on its own and largely through "technological solutions." Union Minister for Electronics and Information Technology Ravi Shankar Prasad (who also holds the Law portfolio in the Council of Ministers) first demanded that Facebook check the spread of fake news in September

2016. Since then he has repeated this demand several times over.

He said: "There is a need for bringing in traceability and accountability when a provocative/inflammatory message is detected and a request is made by law enforcement agencies. When rumours and fake news get propagated by mischief mongers, the medium used for such propagation cannot evade responsibility and accountability. If they remain mute spectators they are liable to be treated as abettors and thereafter face consequent legal action."

That month, for the first time, the Indian government demanded "traceability" of senders of messages on WhatsApp. Two notices were sent by the Ministry of Electronics and Information Technology (MEITY) to the organisation in quick succession. Between May and July 2018, there had been at least three gruesome killings after fake messages were circulated on WhatsApp.

In May 2018, a 26-year-old labourer from Rajasthan who was working in Bengaluru, the country's "IT (information technology) capital," was lynched apparently after a fake video had been doing the rounds claiming that persons from outside Karnataka were "stealing" children.

In Maharashtra's Dhule district, five persons were lynched in July 2018 after fake videos were shared on WhatsApp groups claiming that a gang was "harvesting organs" of dead children – one video from 2013 depicted children who had died after a nerve-gas attack in Syria. The superintendent of police of the district told *Wired* magazine how addicted local people had become to using the social media platform on their mobile phones and sardonically remarked that some of them could live without oxygen but not WhatsApp.

The same month, a 32-year-old Muslim software engineer was brutally lynched by a mob in Bidar, Karnataka, after fake videos about children being kidnapped had been distributed on WhatsApp.

A year earlier, in June 2017, 55-year-old meat trader Alimuddin Ansari had been lynched by a mob of vigilantes for allegedly transporting beef illegally in Ramgarh, Jharkhand. His helpless wife and son learnt about his killing almost in real time on WhatsApp. A year later, Harvard-educated Union Civil Aviation Minister Jayant Sinha was photographed garlanding some of those who had been accused of being part of the lynch mob (and who were out of prison on bail) at his home in Hazaribagh. Sinha, who is member of the Lok Sabha from the constituency, later expressed regret for what he did.

In July 2018, Minister Prasad said that while the government of India does not want to read everyone's messages on WhatsApp it was not rocket science for Facebook to use technology, artificial intelligence and machine learning to curb the mass circulation of false information. He added that while social media platforms like WhatsApp can be commercially successful, it must at the same time be accountable, responsible and vigilant. He said the measures taken by WhatsApp to tackle the circulation of fake news did not meet the government's expectations on "traceability."

A spokesperson of WhatsApp promptly responded and said the platform "cares deeply about people's safety," that it was working with Indian researchers to address the problem of proliferation of fake news and would run public safety campaigns. Soon thereafter, WhatsApp placed a forwarded tag to indicate that a message had been forwarded and restricted the number of individual users or groups to which a message could be forwarded at one go to five.

After WhatsApp's global head Chris Daniels met Prasad on 30 October – his second visit to India in as many months – a spokesperson of the organisation stated: "We appreciate the opportunity to meet with government leaders, including Minister Prasad who confirmed his support for encryption and the privacy of our users. WhatsApp is deeply committed to serving the people of India and (is) working closely with civil society and government leaders to help address abuse on our platform."

An aside: *Daniels is reportedly very upset with the government of India but for reasons that have nothing to do with fake news and hate speech on WhatsApp. A person who met him said on condition of anonymity, "He was livid that WhatsApp had not been granted permission to start its payments gateway although he claimed that his organisation had fulfilled all the conditions that PayTM and Google Pay had."*

In this context, he told The Economic Times *that it was "critical that Indian leaders ensure a level playing-field."*

The Reserve Bank of India, the country's central bank and apex monetary authority, has argued that WhatsApp has not agreed to conditions relating to "data localisation" or the storing of all relevant data on financial transactions in servers located within the country.

On issues of encryption and traceability, Daniels was categorical that WhatsApp should remain the way it was built, namely, as "a place for private conversations" – and that it could not provide information about the originator of content unless its systems were redesigned and its privacy standards revised to enable it to "indiscriminately track user data."

Daniels added that while "relying on law enforcement is not enough," there was need for "broad education to explain how to stay safe" which, in turn, was the job of every stakeholder, technology companies, civil society and the government.

An independent observer like Mishi Chaudhary, legal director of the Software Freedom Law Centre and a digital rights activist who divides her time between New Delhi and New York, is of the view that Facebook could have done much more to ensure that users are not made part of groups without their prior consent – this was before WhatsApp updated its privacy settings in April 2019. She said: "Like all technology companies, Facebook believes that every problem can be solved by more technology but things are not always that simple."

Chaudhary says messages not only impact the conscious mind but unconsciously influence people as well, especially in view of the highly-addictive nature of social media platforms like Facebook and Twitter. "You keep spamming a falsehood and after a while, some people start believing the untruth – it's a classic 'Goebbelsian' technique," she said in a reference to Paul Joseph Goebbels, a close associate of Adolf Hitler and propaganda minister in Nazi Germany between 1933 and 1945.

Chinmayi Arun, a fellow at the Berkman Klein Center, Harvard University, and founder director of the Centre for Communication Governance at the National Law University, Delhi, has asserted in an article titled, "On WhatsApp, Rumours and Lynchings," published in the *Economic and Political Weekly* that: "The Indian government is treating the lynchings as a 'fake news' problem, and is placing the onus of remedies on

WhatsApp. This is a misdirected policy response that does little to address the issue."

She draws a distinction between disinformation and incitement to violence, and claims WhatsApp's willingness to cooperate with the Indian government has potential to lead to human rights abuses:

"In the context of the lynchings, it is helpful to think of the rumours as a form of incitement to violence. This particular form may need to be treated differently since much of Indian hate speech jurisprudence is criminal law, and tends to focus on the speaker or on pre-censorship of speech (Arun and Nayak 2016). Criminalisation is a questionable approach since the nature of viral rumours on social media is such that the person who authored content might not have anticipated whom it might reach and what effect it might have on them. Consider, for example, a person from Kerala who reports truthfully that children are being kidnapped in her village, and finds that her speech resulted in a lynching after being shared out of context by a third party in a different village in Uttar Pradesh. It would hardly be fair to hold such a person responsible for the lynching. This is not to say that authors always lack the intention to incite violence, or the knowledge that their content will be circulated among people who might see it as a call for action. It does, however, raise questions about whether the rumours are incitement to violence inherently, or whether they become so in the context in which they are shared.

"The other good reason to question all solutions that veer towards identifying the speaker is that this may have serious implications for privacy and for freedom of expression. Facebook, for example, has incorrectly flagged the phrase 'Free

Kashmir' as locally illegal content for censorship purposes, when it is in fact constitutionally protected speech. Such a practice affects the rights of the Kashmiri people who already find themselves without a voice or a platform since Kashmir sees extensive media censorship and disruption of internet services. If WhatsApp were to adopt Facebook's broad definitions of illegal speech, it might contribute to the violation of the international human rights of privacy and freedom of expression around the world. For example, identifying the speaker may endanger a young woman who shares her 'MeToo' story about a powerful man in a WhatsApp group of trusted friends. Currently, such stories go viral without the woman's identity being compromised.

"This means that we need to consider other ways to cope with this burgeoning problem of incitement to violence on WhatsApp that do not necessarily involve identifying the original content creator. Once we let go of the idea that the original speaker must be traced, policy suggestions involving the disabling of anonymous forwards on social media, breaking encryption and otherwise violating privacy to trace the source of speech become unnecessary.

"WhatsApp's role in the violence may be that it is used to amplify and target harmful speech. It is not clear how access to metadata, encrypted communication, or identification of speakers is expected to mitigate the larger problem, since rumours lead to lynchings even without WhatsApp playing an intermediary role. Ironically enough, it may be WhatsApp's misguided cooperation with the Indian government following the bad publicity for the lynchings that may eventually lead to the large scale violation of human rights in India."

Facebook's critics say it only pays lip-service to tackling the spread of fake information. Its entire business model is predicated on posts becoming viral. The more a user interacts with the platform and gets hooked on to it, the better for Facebook. "The company is treating fake news as a public relations problem in India," says Pratik Sinha, co-founder of *AltNews*, adding: "There are many ways to deal with disinformation but that is not a priority for the bosses at Facebook. For them, it is at best a tick-box exercise response."

It has been well documented by fact-checking websites like *AltNews* and *BOOMLive* that supporters of Modi and the BJP have been serial offenders as far as propagating disinformation is concerned. One such right-wing website is *Postcard News* co-founded by Mahesh Hegde. He was arrested by the Bengaluru police on 30 March 2018 for alleging that a Jain monk had been assaulted by a Muslim man whereas the individual had suffered minor injuries in a road accident. Union Minister Anantkumar Hegde (not related to Mahesh Hegde) called for his release and described his arrest as "politically motivated." The website of *Postcard News* has in the past been accused of spreading disinformation about, among others, television journalist Barkha Dutt and West Bengal Chief Minister Mamata Banerjee. It is replete with pro-BJP propaganda.

Whereas Mahesh Hedge's arrest was a rare instance of police action against a peddler of problematic information, what has caused considerable consternation is how a large number of users of social media platforms like Facebook and Twitter who have been accused of spreading disinformation continue to be "followed" by the Prime Minister and other ministers in the Union government.

When questioned by one of the writers of this book as to why Modi was not "unfollowing" or "unfriending" regular disseminators of disinformation at a conference in Jaipur on 11 October, Suresh Kochattil, adviser, Information Technology Cell of the BJP in Telangana, said it was not realistic to expect a person like the Prime Minister of India, who has millions of followers on the social media, to keep track about who is spreading fake news and who should not be followed or befriended. At the same conference, he had concluded his presentation on "political wars on social media" by remarking that "things are going to get worse" in the approach to the forthcoming general elections "before they get better."

A Facebook page titled *Jay Modiraj* (or "hail Modi's rule") with 1.4 million followers and which ran an advertising campaign in 2018 to garner more "likes," has been very active circulating manipulated images of the Prime Minister, trashing his political opponents and encouraging Islamophobia. One set of two pictures depicted Modi with yellow and red marks on his forehead next to Congress President Rahul Gandhi wearing a Muslim skullcap. As reported by *AltNews*, the captions in Hindi read: "One fights for truth, the other advocates terrorism."[1]

The same page had published and circulated reports from a disinformation website called "BBCNewsHub" that stated that the Congress was the world's fourth most corrupt party and

---

1   https://www.altnews.in/the-faces-behind-facebook-page-jay-modiraj-a-factory-of-hate-and-misinformation/

that Sonia Gandhi was the world's fourth richest woman. This Facebook page also posted manipulated pictures of Modi with world leaders, false quotes of Indian Army chief Bipin Rawat and Congress MP Shashi Tharoor calling Modi a scorpion and incorrect information about World Bank loans to India. On the Facebook page of *Jay Modiraj*, there is a picture from Thailand that was sought to be passed off as a military drill being conducted in India. It also circulated a manipulated image of Modi standing next to former Prime Minister Atal Behari Vajpayee's body.

The fact-checking website *AltNews* investigated the individuals associated with the page – Sachin Patel, Rajesh Soni, Bhavin Patel, Manoj Gilani and Neha Patel – and found that most of them had "display pictures" or DPs of themselves with Prime Minister Modi and some had attended a meeting organised for the Prime Minister to interact with his party's social media volunteers. One among the persons named (Bhavin Patel) described himself on Facebook as a member of the IT Cell of the BJP and the Rashtriya Swayamsevak Sangh (RSS).

More such egregious instances will be cited later.

The fact is that some trolls who claim to be supporters of the ruling party have become akin to Dr Frankenstein's Monster and have ended up embarrassing the Modi government. In July 2018, External Affairs Minister Sushma Swaraj was viciously trolled and abused on social media platforms in connection with the issuance of passports to an inter-faith couple in Lucknow. The filthy language used against her elicited an anguished response from her husband Swaraj Kaushal.

WhatsApp was reportedly "misused" for a different kind

of "lynching" of a financial nature. The share prices of a publicly-listed company, Infibeam, collapsed by as much as 71 per cent on a single day (28 September 2018) following a WhatsApp message that had raised concerns about the e-commerce company's allegedly dodgy accounting practices. The incident made headlines in the financial media.

As we approached many individuals about Facebook and WhatsApp, including current and former employees of Facebook India, we realised that many of them did not want to be quoted fearing repercussions. It became evident to us that key individuals involved with the organisation share an uncomfortably close relationship with the BJP and at least one of them was associated with Modi's pre-election campaign in 2013 and 2014 and was supporting a website that spread pro-BJP news on Facebook. We also looked into what appeared to be an instance of "conflict of interest" involving a senior functionary of Facebook India. There's much more to come in the following chapters.

3

Facebook Helps Modi

Is Facebook truly an agnostic platform for all to use? We don't think it is. The evidence we collated indicated that certain senior employees of Facebook India have worked, and continue to work, very closely with India's ruling party. Their close links with the BJP existed well before Modi became Prime Minister in May 2014 and got strengthened thereafter. Facebook has a track record across the world of working closely with those in power, including with authoritarian rulers.

In September 2017, the President of the United States of America Donald Trump accused Facebook of bias against him. The chief executive officer of the world's biggest social media platform Mark Zuckerberg stated:

I want to respond to President Trump's Tweet... claiming Facebook has always been against him. Every day I work to bring people together and build a community for everyone. We hope to give all people a voice and create a platform for all ideas. Trump says Facebook is against him. Liberals say we helped Trump. Both sides are upset about ideas and content they don't like. That's what running a platform for all ideas looks like… This was the first US election where the internet was a primary way candidates communicated. Every candidate had a Facebook page to communicate directly with tens of millions of followers every day. Campaigns spent hundreds of millions advertising online to get their messages out even further. That's 1,000x more than any problematic ad(vertisement)s we've found…

After the election, I made a comment that I thought the idea misinformation on Facebook changed the outcome of the election was a crazy idea. Calling that crazy was dismissive and I regret it. This is too important an issue to be dismissive. But the data we have has always shown that our broader impact − from giving people a voice to enabling candidates to communicate directly to helping millions of people vote − played a far bigger role in this election… We will do our part to defend against nation-states attempting to spread misinformation and subvert elections. We'll keep working to ensure the integrity of free and fair elections around the world, and to ensure our community is a platform for all ideas and (a) force for good in democracy.

How sincere was Zuckerberg? Or was he merely mouthing platitudes in reaction to growing criticism of Facebook and its failure to check abuse and manipulation of its ostensibly-agnostic social media platform by interest groups? A few months later, in December 2017, *Bloomberg* published a report authored by Laurence Etter, Vernon Silver and Sarah Frier titled "How Facebook's Political Unit Enables the Dark Art of Digital Propaganda." The article categorically asserted that the company and its employees work "… actively with political parties and leaders who use Facebook to stifle opposition – sometimes with the aid of 'troll armies' that spread misinformation and extremist ideologies."

The report added that members of the team led by Katie Harbath, global politics and government outreach director of Facebook, who had earlier worked as a digital strategist with the Republican Party and with former New York Mayor Rudy Giuliani, had worked as "*de facto* campaign managers" for politicians in India, Brazil, Germany, the United Kingdom, Argentina, Poland, the Philippines. They reportedly supported "patriotic trolling" or used government-backed propaganda to harass dissidents and consolidate power. The *Bloomberg* article quoted Mark Crispin Miller, media and cultural studies professor at New York University saying: "They're (meaning Facebook's employees are) too cosy with power."

Facebook helped Narendra Modi develop his online presence to ensure that he has more "followers" on the social media platform than any other political leader on the planet. According to a study called "World Leaders on Facebook" by Burson Cohn and Wolfe, in May 2018, Modi had as many as 43.2 million "followers" on the platform with Trump coming a poor second with 23.1 million followers.

From the day elections were announced in March 2014 till the day the polling ended, 29 million people in India made 227 million interactions (posts, comments, shares and likes) regarding the Indian elections on Facebook. This number was approximately two-thirds the number of daily active Facebook users in India and worked out to an average of ten interactions per person. In addition, 13 million people made 75 million interactions specifically regarding Modi.

In his 2019 book titled *How to Win An Indian Election: What Political Parties Don't Want You to Know* published by Penguin Random House India, 25-year-old political activist Shivam Shankar Singh (who was with the BJP before falling out with the party) pointed out how in August 2018, Modi and the BJP were far ahead of Rahul Gandhi and the Indian National Congress (INC) in terms of followers on social media platforms: the BJP had 14.6 million followers on Facebook against 4.8 million for the Congress; Modi had 42.7 million followers whereas Rahul Gandhi had 1.8 million. The difference in the number of followers the two parties and the two leaders had on YouTube and Twitter were equally stark.

Singh wrote that it was only in 2016 that the BJP realised the huge potential of WhatsApp to shape political preferences and became "a major part of the party's arsenal." He quotes the BJP's IT cell head Amit Malviya telling *The Economic Times*: "The upcoming elections will be fought on the mobile phone… In a way, you could say they would be WhatsApp elections."

He pointed out that the BJP was "looking beyond WhatsApp" and is aggressively promoting an application named after Narendra Modi. The NaMo App had over five million downloads on the Android App Store by April 2018 and was one of the few third-party applications available for download on the For consistency word App is with capital 'a', as a mix is used store of Reliance Jio – whose launch in August 2016 saw the company headed by India's richest man Mukesh Ambani place prominent advertisements of the mobile phone and data service using the Prime Minister's beaming visage. The NaMo App is prebuilt into Reliance Jio as well as other low-cost Indian smartphones, including those that had been distributed free before the November–December 2018 Assembly elections in Chhattisgarh and Rajasthan. More about the NaMo App is detailed later in the book.

With the People's Republic of China shutting Facebook out of the world's most-populous country, India has been – and will continue to remain – the digital monopoly's biggest market in terms of number of users. Its platforms, including WhatsApp and Instagram, comprise an unparalleled and unprecedented backbone of an internet-based communications infrastructure. India, with over 1.3 billion people – with a median age of 27 and half the population below the age of 26 – had the largest number of WhatsApp users in the world at the end of 2018 at not less than 250 million – some contend that this number is on the low side and that the actual number is perhaps 300 million or more. For some years now, the largest number of users of Facebook is also from India.

From an estimated 100 million in 2014, the number of users of Facebook went up to 136 million the following year. By April 2018, the total number of users of Facebook and WhatsApp had exceeded 200 million and rose further to over 220 million till September. Some would place these estimates as conservative. One "guess-estimate" places the number of current Facebook users at 270 million. The number of users in India is projected to go up to somewhere in the region of 300 million by 2022. The current number of Instagram users in India at 64 million is the fourth highest in the world.

India has also emerged as the biggest disinformation factory in the world in recent years. The digital footprint of Indian companies, many close to the ruling regime, have been reported in at least five countries, including the US and Mexico, that have witnessed elections over the last few years. There is good reason to believe that the social media, after being extensively used during the assembly elections in five states in November–December 2018, is being deployed on a larger scale in the April–May 2019 general elections.

Flashback: *In April 2013, a study by IRIS Knowledge Foundation and the Internet and Mobile Association of India had claimed that the social media, notably Facebook, could influence the outcome of as many 160 "high impact" Lok Sabha constituencies out of the 543 in the country. At that time, many scoffed at this claim. However, there is no denying the fact that over the last six years, the use of the social media, especially WhatsApp, has expanded manifold and political leaders cutting across party affiliation believe that what is being put out over the social media in the coming months could have a significant influence in shaping voting preferences across India, not just in urban areas but even in small towns and in rural areas as well.*

While there are multiple views on the efficacy of social media and psychographic targeting, it is well-established that in constituencies where there are close contests, social media can play a role in determining electoral outcomes. Praveen Chakravarty, economist and former investment banker who was appointed as head of data analytics at the Indian National Congress in February, has described the outcome of the 2014 general elections as a "black swan" moment as the BJP won 282 out of 543 seats in the Lok Sabha with 31.4 per cent of the popular vote. As much as 90 per cent of all the votes obtained by the party was concentrated in roughly

60 per cent of the Parliamentary constituencies (to be precise, 299 Lok Sabha constituencies) with the remaining 10 per cent spread over the remaining 40 per cent or 254 constituencies.

With the 17th general elections more keenly contested than the one in 2014, the imperative to "weaponise" social media evidently became more important than ever before for India's political parties.

4

Exponential Growth

Facebook opened its first office in India in 2011. At that time, the platform had 15 million users in the country and was still three years away from buying WhatsApp. Its office in Hyderabad was staffed mostly by sales personnel. A year later, Facebook appointed Ankhi Das as its Policy Director for India. Before joining Facebook, she had worked as the communications head at Microsoft India and had excellent relations with politicians, bureaucrats and policy-makers. She was considered "perfect for the job."

India was then in the midst of social turmoil and political uncertainty. A nationwide anti-corruption movement had started in 2011 and the gang-rape of a young woman in the heart of the country's capital in 2012 had stirred middle-class Indians to come out on the streets. The country was witnessing protests by ordinary citizens on a scale not seen for decades. The BJP, which was then the principal opposition party, was disrupting proceedings in Parliament. The media was relentlessly focussing on stories of big-ticket corruption involving important functionaries in the Congress-led United

Progressive Alliance coalition government. To many political observers, the Manmohan Singh government appeared to be on its last legs after ruling the country since 2004.

Two years after opening its office, Facebook had fast turned into a platform of choice for political conversations online and for mobilising people, especially young adults, to support a variety of causes, notably political ones. The company nearly doubled its users in India from 15 million in 2011 to 28 million the following year. Much of this growth came from users between the ages of 17 and 35.

In October 2014, Facebook founder Zuckerberg arrived at Chandrauli village in Haryana in an orange helicopter to see first-hand how the internet and the use of social media could change the lives of ordinary Indians. On that trip, he met Prime Minister Modi in New Delhi and exulted about his "Digital India" initiative. A few months later, in March 2015, Facebook enthusiastically rolled out its internet.org plan to provide "free" access to some three-dozen selected websites. A Reliance group company, which provided the service, put out advertisements that read: "The sun is free. The air is free. Then why shouldn't the internet be free?"

Facebook did not anticipate then that the scheme would be rejected by the citizens of the country as a "gift they did not need." The regulatory body, the Telecom Regulatory Authority of India (TRAI) asked for public comments on Facebook's offer which was re-christened "Free Basics" – using the same acronym as the parent organisation. Opposition had started building up to the "gift" that was being offered. An instance of the resistance was reflected in the popularity of the video of a show by the satirical group All India Bakchod ridiculing the "FB" scheme which got over 3.5 million views. Still, Facebook persisted. Thousands of billboards were put up across the country. Front pages of leading newspapers advertised Free Basics. Big bucks were being spent. The publicity campaign is supposed to have cost the company over ₹250 crore.

In September 2015, after Modi hugged Zuckerberg to much applause at a townhall meeting at Facebook's headquarters in Menlo Park in California's Silicon Valley, Facebook's promoter put out a post that read: "In recent campaigns around the world – from India and Indonesia across Europe to the United States – we've seen the candidate with the largest following on Facebook usually wins."

In barely a month, Zuckerberg was back in India addressing entrepreneurs using the internet at the prestigious Indian Institute of Technology, Delhi. Media reports suggest that many were sceptical of what Facebook was offering while others were downright hostile to the scheme which would "discriminate" among websites that could be accessed "free" thus violating the tenets of net neutrality – it was akin to telling users of a library that books in only certain sections would be available for reading without payment.

Two days before a TRAI deadline for public responses to questions on net neutrality, Zuckerberg published an editorial page article plugging Free Basics in *The Times of India (ToI)*, India's – and the world's – most widely circulated English daily. Sixteen million users of Facebook were apparently prompted to send messages to TRAI supporting Free Basics.

Apar Gupta, executive director, Internet Freedom

Foundation and a lawyer who has been advocating free speech issues, recalls how he had serious differences – and heated exchanges – with Facebook's representatives, including Das, about the organisation's lobbying methods. "Me and others told them (representatives of Facebook) that this was not the way to put their views across to the government, but they went ahead," he said.

All the efforts put in by Facebook were, however, in vain. The Free Basics programme, which had apparently been "welcomed" in countries like Colombia, Ghana, Kenya, Nigeria, Mexico, Pakistan and the Philippines, was summarily rejected by India's telecom regulator TRAI – a move that was welcomed by digital activists in the country. On 8 February 2016, Facebook stopped the Free Basics scheme in India.

Soon there was to be a change of guard in Facebook India. Umang Bedi joined as vice-president and managing director in June 2016. He did not last long. Fifteen months later, in October 2017, he quit and was replaced by Sandeep Bhushan.

Earlier, in May that year, Facebook launched its Express WiFi initiative in partnership with telecommunications group Bharti Airtel to set up 20,000 wifi hotspots across India.

We reached out to Bedi for his comments, but he declined to speak citing a confidentiality agreement with his former employer. (He is now based out of Bengaluru and heads *Daily Hunt* which is engaged in promoting news feeds in Indian languages other than English.)

During the period Facebook was actively lobbying for Free Basics, Zuckerberg, his second-in-command Sheryl Sandberg and other top executives were actively assisted by Ankhi Das who was heading policy and government relations in India for the organisation. Writing in the UK-based *The Guardian* in May 2016, journalist Rahul Bhatia quoted an unnamed Facebook executive saying: "We used to joke that she (Das) was like Modi's grand-daughter." The big storm was to come subsequently.

The past two years (2017 and 2018) have been pretty hellish for Facebook. The organisation has faced increased international scrutiny and strident criticism. It has come to epitomise all things that have gone wrong with the technology industry. Its platforms have been accused of helping manipulate public opinion to influence elections, trigger violence, censoring news and covertly assisting regimes to consolidate more power. Facebook's executives have been censured for allegedly misleading sovereign governments on its business practices and user policies. There have been calls for the resignation of Zuckerberg and his deputy Sandberg.

It has been argued that the time has come for the digital giant to be considered a monopoly and broken up in the manner in which the Bell Group or AT&T – once known as the American Telephone and Telegraph Company, founded in 1879 by Alexander Graham Bell who invented the telephone – was fragmented into competing entities in the early-1980s. Among those who are advocating for a fragmentation of Facebook, Google and Amazon is Elizabeth Warren, US Presidential hopeful from the Democratic Party. The Senator blogged: "Today's big tech companies have too much power – too much power over our economy, our society, and our democracy... They've bulldozed competition, used our private information for profit, and tilted the playing field against everyone else."

In September 2018, a United Nations organisation recommended an independent investigation into the company's complicity in the genocide of Rohingyas in Myanmar. The company acknowledged that it should have acted much before it did.

Unlike in other countries, criticism of Facebook's activities has been relatively muted in India. Its close association with the ruling party and the incumbent regime has been of great help in this regard. As we shall subsequently detail, a key official of Facebook India in an earlier avatar had a close association with Modi's pre-election campaign in 2013. An organisation helmed by this person's wife has been supported by Facebook in what has been alleged as an instance of "conflict of interest," a contention that was denied by a spokesperson of the organisation. But more about these facts later.

Little is publicly known about Facebook India's relationships with political parties, unlike what has been disclosed about the role the organisation supposedly played in supporting the campaign that saw Trump becoming President of the US in November 2016 and the alleged Russian collaboration in the campaign to elect him. Four years earlier, in 2012, Barack Obama's use of social media had been much commented on. He was affectionately described as the world's first "Facebook President."

In late-2002, the western Indian state of Gujarat was headed for an election for its legislative assembly. The state was the stronghold of Modi and the BJP. After the anti-Muslim riots in the state earlier that year, Modi was very keen on projecting his "pro-industry" and "pro-technology" image. He was himself beginning to realise the potential of digital media in garnering political support. The role that Facebook and WhatsApp would play in influencing political opinion was not realised till much later.

An article in the *Ken* portal published on 6 February 2019 sought to answer the question: Exactly how big is Facebook is in India? Written by Ashish K Mishra, the article explained why so little is known about the organisation's finances in the country. From late-2018, Facebook stated that it would be recording all its advertising revenue in India in order to comply with the newly-introduced Goods and Services Tax. A firm named Facebook India Online Services Private Limited saw its revenues rising to ₹521 crore ($72.7 million) from ₹341 crore ($47.5 million) between financial years 2016–17 and 2017–18, with profits rising from ₹40 crore ($5.5 million) to ₹57 crore ($8 million) in this period. The numbers seem very low, Mishra observed, because "Facebook made $40 billion in annual revenue in 2017 globally with a net profit of $16 billion... To imagine then, that India, with close to 294 million users – Facebook's largest user base anywhere in the world – would not even contribute 1 per cent to the company's total revenue... well, that just seems improbable" especially in comparison to its rival Google.

Facebook did not provide too many details to *Ken*. Mishra identified a few companies that may be associated with Facebook in India (like Communiti Connect Private

Limited and Oceantis Services Private Limited) but was not sure. It was observed that the group possibly books a part of its revenues outside India. The article quoted unnamed sources claiming that Facebook and its sister platforms, WhatsApp and Instagram, perhaps clocked a total annual turnover in the region of ₹3,000 crore (or over $400 million).

5

Role of Rajesh Jain

At a private meeting in April 2010, Rajesh Jain, an internet millionaire from Mumbai made a power-point presentation to the then Chief Minister of Gujarat titled "Prime Minister Narendra Modi, 2014." Four months later, Jain was appointed director of Gujarat Informatics Limited, a state government-owned information technology (IT) company. Over the next three years, with a clutch of other entrepreneurs, bankers, journalists and members of the BJP's IT cell, Jain helped execute what can be described as one of the most elaborate political marketing exercises of its kind in modern India, an exercise that the BJP's critics describe as developing "myths" surrounding Modi's persona.

Jain had plans of his own. He had studied electrical and communications engineering at the Indian Institute of Technology in Mumbai and at Columbia University, New York. In 1993, Jain made headlines while analysing photographic evidence that contradicted the Indian government's defence of former Prime Minister P V Narasimha Rao's alleged involvement in a bribery case. It had been claimed that

Narasimha Rao had received a bribe of ₹1 crore from Mumbai-based stockbroker Harshad Mehta who was at the epicentre of a major financial scandal. The Prime Minister's Office (PMO) predictably denied the claim. And to rubbish Mehta, it put out a photograph of Narasimha Rao with the then External Affairs Minister of Pakistan and claimed that the Prime Minister was meeting the Pakistan minister at precisely the time the broker had alleged that he had paid the bribe to him.

Jain analysed an image published in *India Today* magazine and conclusively proved that the PMO was lying.[2] The source mentioned in the report was Ravi Database Consultants Private Limited, then headed by Jain.

After a second trip to the US in late-1994 where he experienced first-hand the huge potential of the internet, in March 1995, he started IndiaWorld which was supposed to be the country's "first" digital media company, or so he contended. Jain hit the proverbial jackpot less than five years later in December 1999 when Satyam Infoway brought IndiaWorld Communications for ₹499 crore in cash, then equivalent to US$115 million. By then, India World had evolved from operating a single website – to an internet services company that hosted websites, mail servers and search engines. It ran a family of nine websites across news, sports, entertainment, horoscopes and astrology, personal finance, history and food. IndiaWorld, at that time, had recorded an

---

2   https://www.indiatoday.in/magazine/special-report/ story/19930731-elusive-truth-pms-defence-against-harshad- mehtas-allegations-full-of-holes-811354-1993-07-31.

impressive 13 million page-views. Its clientele was mostly non-resident Indians (NRIs).

After the sale, Jain worked with Satyam Infoway for the next two years. In 2001, he took control over Netcore Solutions, the firm that oversaw the software and enterprise solutions business of IndiaWorld that did not go under the hammer. Today, Netcore claims it is the biggest digital marketing and campaign management solution provider of its kind in the country, and arguably among the biggest in the world. During this period, Jain reportedly had his second and most impactful brush with politics in India.

The BJP was looking for an SMS (short-messaging service) vendor in January 2009. That brought him in touch with Piyush Goyal, the current Union Minister for Railways. His company bagged the contract and days later, Jain (who belongs to a family that has supported the BJP for generations) teamed up with a bunch of people, including former banker Amit Malviya (who now heads the BJP's IT cell), lawyer Hitesh Jain and others, to start a group of called "Friends of BJP." This group was started in January 2009 to engage middle-class citizens and get them to support Modi. The group's initial efforts did not yield any significant results for the BJP. In May that year, the BJP-led National Democratic Alliance lost the 15th general elections.

After almost a year, following a private meeting with Modi in April 2010, Jain got down to work with renewed vigour. He wanted to engineer a "wave election" for Modi to ensure a majority for the BJP in the 2014 general elections, as he himself wrote in a public blog post at www.emergic.org in June 2011. That year, the pace picked up after he had multiple meetings with Modi and was introduced to Dr Hiren Joshi, Modi's proverbial Man Friday in Gujarat. Joshi had been hand-picked by Modi to work with him in Gujarat after 18 years of teaching; he is currently Officer on Special Duty or OSD in charge of information technology in the PMO in New Delhi and, as will be subsequently elaborated upon, an extremely influential technocrat whose writ extends beyond information technology.

Jain started by launching NITI Digital, NITI being an acronym for New Initiatives to Transform India – the meaning of *niti* in Hindi, depending on its usage, is either policy or ethics. (Incidentally, the Planning Commission's new avatar is NITI Aayog and in this instance, NITI stands for National Institution for Transforming India.) One of Jain's key initiatives was *NitiCentral.com*, a pro-BJP news and opinions site, with journalist Kanchan Gupta as the editorial head. Gupta had earlier worked in the PMO in the Atal Behari Vajpayee government with the then National Security Adviser Brajesh Mishra and had later headed the Maulana Azad Centre for Indian Culture in Cairo, Egypt.

In the coming years, *NitiCentral* would become one of the biggest online influencers of political opinion in favour of Modi. Jain also launched a volunteering platform, *India272.com* – the figure 272 is the half-way mark of the number of seats in the Lok Sabha – with support from B G Mahesh (a technology entrepreneur from Bengaluru) and Shashi Shekhar Vempati, who had at that juncture recently quit Infosys and returned to India from the US. (Shekhar is currently heading the government-owned broadcaster Prasar Bharati Corporation which runs Doordarshan and All India Radio.) Jain was later a part of the "Mission 272+" initiative in the run-up to the 16th general elections that took place in April–May 2014.

We contacted Rajesh Jain to speak about the pivotal role he reportedly played in designing and spearheading Modi's online and social media campaign. He, however, declined to be interviewed.

Former television anchor with *NDTV* Shivnath Thukral (who was then working with the Essar group controlled by the Ruia family, before he went on to join the Carnegie Foundation in India and thereafter, Facebook India) along with an investment banker, Anuj Gupta, helped Hiren Joshi create and run *Mera Bharosa* (literally translated to mean "My Trust") and other web pages for the BJP. Gupta, a long-time associate of Piyush Goyal is at present OSD to the Union Minister for Railways. More about these key players – Katie Harbath of Facebook in the US, Thukral of Facebook India, Hiren Joshi in the Prime Minister's Office, Anuj Gupta in Railway Minister Goyal's office and others come later in this book.

A very important initiative that Mumbai-based technology entrepreneur Rajesh Jain spearheaded for Narendra Modi and the BJP in the run-up to the April–May 2014 general elections was the construction of an ambitious database of voters which could be used to target messages for users on the social media, specifically WhatsApp and Facebook. Huge volumes of data were scraped from public sources, including electoral rolls and polling booth forms of the Election Commission of India. The idea was to "geo-fence" areas and map vote-swings. By collating names and analysing voting patterns from publicly-available data, Jain's team was able to help the BJP identify strong and weak constituencies across the country, all the way down to the level of the voting booth.

What was truly amazing about this database was that for the first time in India, algorithms were used to finely segment voters not only by caste, geography, location, whether urban, semi-urban or rural but importantly, on the basis of religion. This was of great help to the BJP's social media managers to "micro-target" users of Facebook, WhatsApp and Twitter. "What was never officially disclosed was that an exhaustive and special database was built to identify Muslims and those belonging to other minority communities in the country," said a person conversant with what had happened who spoke to us on condition of anonymity, adding: "Thus, the party's social media managers also knew who *not* to target."

Later, Jain's team started layering the data with mobile phone numbers and linked these with the BJP's "missed call" campaigns across the country. Voters who expressed support for Modi and his party through a missed call were sent a short message on their mobile phones requesting them to send their voter identification details. Many did, and this ensured that the team could target BJP supporters on the day elections would take place to make sure they turned out to vote. (After the elections, Jain's company unsuccessfully tried to market the voter rolls data it had compiled to corporates under the brand name, Radius Code.)

6

An Early Entrant

Narendra Modi had realised the importance of internet and social media well before he became Prime Minister of India in May 2014.

Ten years earlier, on 20 June 2004, the Ahmedabad edition of *The Times of India* carried a report headlined: "Modi Caught in Web Lie." The report stated that the Gujarat government's official website claimed that as a young man, Modi "spearheaded" the Nav Nirman Andolan or the agitation to build society anew that was led by students and political activists in 1974 to oust the "corrupt" Chimanbhai Patel government in Gujarat. During the agitation, over 100 persons had died in police firing. The *ToI* report on the official website had claimed that:

> ... His leadership qualities caught the eyes of several leaders including Shri Jayaprakash Narayan who carried this Andolan against corruption to every nook and corner of the country. However, the real heroes of the movement are furious. Almost all the people who actually spearheaded the movement

unanimously rubbish the claim... Experts say of the few books which talk about the agitation, not one mentions Modi. Vishnu Pandya, who was the editor of (the) RSS (Rashtriya Swayamsevak Sangh) magazine *Sadhana*, wrote two books... which have chapters on (the) Nav Nirman (movement). And none of them has Modi in it.

Nilanjan Mukhopadhyay, journalist and author of *Narendra Modi: The Man, The Times* (Tranquebar, 2013), recalled this article in his book and added:

In the summer of 2012, the URL (or uniform resource locator or web address) link, given by the newspaper led people to Modi's personal website, which Dr Hiren Joshi, his OSD (IT) told me is maintained by "supporters and fans." This profile of Modi that was available at the point of writing (*www. narendramodi.in*) had been modified. Instead of the categorical assertion as claimed by *The Times of India* in its report of 2004, the website had a toned down version: "During his tenure with the RSS, Shri Narendra Modi played several important roles on various occasions including the 1974 Nav Nirman anti-corruption agitation and the harrowing 19-month (June 1975 to January 1977) long 'emergency' when the fundamental rights of Indian citizens were strangled. Modi kept the spirit of democracy alive by going underground for the entire period and fighting a spirited battle against the fascist ways of the then central government."

Mukhopadhyay wrote that in 2012, Modi, who was the Chief Minister of Gujarat, had tweeted: "Every morning I share an inspiring quote of Swami Vivekananda on his 150th anniversary. I request media friends not to misquote it for TRPs (or television rating points)." The tweet had come because certain news television channels had given a political spin to the Vivekananda quote that stated: "Will is caused by character, and character by Karma. As is Karma, so is the manifestation of the will."

The quote had been interpreted contentiously because a few days earlier, the Chief Minister of Bihar Nitish Kumar had stated that the prime ministerial candidate of the BJP-led NDA coalition should be a person with "secular credentials and should be acceptable to all sections of the society" and it was at that stage unclear that Modi would become the BJP's candidate for the post of prime minister. This was the year of the 150th birth anniversary of Vivekananda, who is revered by many Indians, and Modi was seeking to circumvent the provisions of the Model Code of Conduct (MCC) that had come into force before the elections to the Gujarat state assembly in 2012.

Here are few long excerpts from Mukhopadhyay's book that he provided us:

...Modi had authorized a daily quote of Vivekananda. Since Modi's Twitter handle – @narendramodi is not "official property" of the state government like the website, *www. narendramodi.in* – it did not cease to function during the election campaign in 2012, like other Twitter accounts or publicity websites which had to adhere to the Election Commission's (Model) Code of Conduct. As a result, Vivekananda quotes were tweeted daily. This episode underscored... that social media had become a very important component in Modi's propaganda and publicity machinery.

… On 1 February 2009, less than three years after the launch of Twitter, Modi began using the social networking platform using the @narendramodi handle. The first tweet was a simple announcement of his visit next day to Dahod 'for Gujarat Swarnim Jayanti Yatra' (or journey to celebrate the golden jubilee of the formation of the Gujarat state). Less than a fortnight later, Modi launched the Gujarati version of his personal website – www.narendramodi.in. Initially, the tweets were not daily and did not have many followers but right from the beginning, the Tweets were not just announcements of his tours but made for engaging reading. Sample this: "Women would play a crucial role in the development of Gujarat" – a Tweet would say and then give a link to the complete speech on the topic; "Through water conservation movement, Kutch has an extraordinary ability to replicate Israel" – another speech of his. Early in his life as a Twitteratti, Modi also gave links to pure data which underscored development during his tenure – "Gujarat posts 12.8 per cent agriculture growth, highest in India."

By the middle of 2012, Modi had a significant presence in cyberspace. Besides Twitter, Modi was also on Google Plus, Facebook and had a channel on YouTube. There are professionals in his team who manage the entire exercise with an OSD on information technology coordinating the entire operation. Political advice has come from colleagues during the election campaign in 2012 but otherwise, it has been his small team. Young professionals were also engaged to bolster the information department of the state government and they work under the direction and guidance of senior officers who personally supervised operations. Modi on his own does not leave everything to his associates, rather he is what is often said about many others – a "hands-on CEO." In terms of Modi's dexterity with gizmos, those who knew him before he became chief minister find one of his practices rather odd: he practically never uses mobile phones after he became chief minister. A source close to Modi explained that "in any case, he is never far from either a landline or from an aide who carried a mobile." The issue became contentious in 2002 when it was alleged that during the riots he had used personal mobile phones of several members of his secretarial staff. The issue dogged him for long and in his deposition to the Special Investigation Team in March 2010 he denied doing so and said that a phone was allotted to him in 2002 but he rarely used it.

While several government departments have been strengthened during Modi's tenure (as Chief Minister of Gujarat), the Information Department has undergone a near-complete overhaul because Modi realizes the power of information and the need for its dissemination more than any other politician in the country. The department has gone shopping for talent in management schools and picked up the best commensurate with competitive wages and is active on Twitter, Facebook, has revamped its website besides of course coming out with an English quarterly journal targeted at embassies. It also runs campaigns on social issues like "Save the Girl Child," "World Environment Day," and against "Trafficking of Women." To stress the fact that Modi took care to ensure that he was not charged of violation of the electoral code of conduct, the Twitter handle of the Information Department, @InfoGujarat suspended tweets on 3 October to resume operations only after the results were officially announced. For Modi, the internet is another platform to publicize his ideas – another theatre for him to demonstrate his skills as a performer. It is not just public meetings that has the audiences for his standout performances – the internet brings them to the computers and now on mobile handsets.

7

Modi's IT Advisers

By the time Rajesh Jain was scaling up his operations in 2013, the BJP's information technology (IT) strategists had begun interacting with social media platforms like Facebook and its partner WhatsApp. If supporters of the BJP are to be believed, the party was better than others in utilising the micro-targeting potential of the platforms. However, it is also true that Facebook's employees in India conducted training workshops to help the members of the BJP's IT cell.

Helping party functionaries were advertising honchos like Sajan Raj Kurup, founder of Creativeland Asia and Prahlad Kakkar, the well-known advertising professional. Actor Anupam Kher became the public face of some of the advertising campaigns. Also assisting the social media and online teams to build a larger-than-life image for Modi before the 2014 elections was a team led by his right-hand man Hiren Joshi, who (as already stated) is a very important adviser to Modi whose writ extends way beyond information technology and social media. Currently, Officer on Special Duty in the Prime Minister's Office, he is assisted by two young professional "techies," Nirav Shah and Yash Rajiv Gandhi. Joshi has had, and continues to have, a close and long-standing association with Facebook's senior employees in India. In 2013, one of his important collaborators was Akhilesh Mishra who later went on to serve as a director of the Indian government's website, MyGov India – which is at present led by Arvind Gupta who was earlier head of the BJP's IT cell. Mishra is CEO of Bluekraft Digital Foundation. The Foundation has been linked to a disinformation website titled "The True Picture," has published books authored by Prime Minister Narendra Modi and produces campaign videos for NaMo Television, a 24 hour cable television channel dedicated to promoting Modi.

The 2014 Modi pre-election campaign was inspired by the 2012 campaign to elect Barack Obama as the "world's first Facebook President." Some of the managers of the Modi campaign like Jain were apparently inspired by Sasha Issenberg's book on the topic, *The Victory Lab: The Secret Science of Winning Campaigns*. In the first data-led election in India in 2014, information was collected from every possible source to not just micro-target users but also fine-tune messages praising and "mythologizing" Modi as the Great Leader who would usher in *acche din* (good times) for the country.

Four teams spearheaded the campaign. The first team was led by Mumbai-based Jain who funded part of the communication campaign and also oversaw voter data analysis. He was helped by Shashi Shekhar Vempati in running NITI and "Mission 272+." As already mentioned, Shekhar had worked in Infosys and is at present the head of Prasar Bharati Corporation which runs Doordarshan and All India Radio.

The second team was led by political strategist Prashant Kishor and his I-PAC or Indian Political Action Committee who supervised the three-dimensional projection programme for Modi besides programmes like Run for Unity, *Chai Pe Charcha* (or Discussions Over Tea), *Manthan* (or Churning) and Citizens for Accountable Governance (CAG) that roped in management graduates to garner support for Modi at large gatherings. Having worked across the political spectrum and opportunistically switched affiliation to those who backed (and paid) him, 41-year-old Kishor is currently the second-in-command in Janata Dal (United) headed by Bihar Chief Minister Nitish Kumar.

The third team, that was intensely focused on building Modi's personal image, was headed by Hiren Joshi himself who worked out of the then Gujarat Chief Minister's Office in Gandhinagar. The members of this team worked closely with staffers of Facebook in India, more than one of our sources told us. As will be detailed later, Shivnath Thukral, who is currently an important executive in Facebook, worked with this team. (We made a number of telephone calls to Joshi's office in New Delhi's South Block seeking a meeting with him and also sent him an email message requesting an interview but he did not respond.)

The fourth team was led by Arvind Gupta, the current CEO of MyGov.in, a social media platform run by the government of India. He ran the BJP's campaign based out of New Delhi. When contacted, he too declined to speak on the record saying he is now with the government and not a representative of the BJP. He suggested we contact Amit Malviya who is the present head of the BJP's IT cell. He came on the line but declined to speak specifically on the BJP's relationship with Facebook and WhatsApp.

The four teams worked separately. "It was (like) a relay (race)," said Vinit Goenka who was then the national co-convener of the BJP's IT cell, adding: "The only knowledge that was shared (among the teams) was on a 'need to know' basis. That's how any sensible organisation works."

From all accounts, Rajesh Jain worked independently from his Lower Parel office and invested his own funds to support Modi and towards executing what he described as "Project 275 for 2014" in a blog post that he wrote in June 2011, nearly three years before the elections actually took place. The BJP, of course, went on to win 282 seats in the 2014 Lok Sabha elections, ten above the half-way mark, with 31 per cent of the votes cast.

As an aside, it may be mentioned in passing that – like certain former bhakts or followers of Modi – Jain today appears less than enthusiastic about the performance of the government. He was engaged in promoting a campaign called Dhan Vapasi *(or "return our wealth") aimed at monetising surplus land and other assets held by government bodies, including defence establishments, and public sector undertakings, for the benefit of the poor and the underprivileged. Dhan Vapasi, in his words, is all about making "every Indian rich and free."*

In one of his recent videos that are in the public domain, Jain remarked: "For the 2014 elections, I had spent three years and my own money to build a team of 100 people to help with Modi's campaign. Why? Because I trusted that a Modi-led BJP government could end the Congress' anti-prosperity programmes and put India on a path to prosperity, a nayi disha *(or new direction). But four years have gone by without any significant change in policy. India needed that to eliminate the big and hamesha (perennial) problems of poverty, unemployment and corruption. The Modi-led BJP government followed the same old failed policy of increasing taxes and spending. The ruler changed, but the outcomes have not."*

As mentioned, when we contacted 51-year-old Jain, who heads the Mumbai-based Netcore group of companies, said to be India's biggest digital media marketing corporate group, he declined to be interviewed. Incidentally, he had till October 2017 served on the boards of directors of two prominent public sector companies. One was National Thermal Power Corporation (NTPC) – Jain has no experience in the power sector, just as Sambit Patra, BJP spokesperson, who is an "independent" director on the board of the Oil and Natural Gas Corporation, has zero experience in the petroleum industry. Jain also served on the board of the Unique Identification Authority of India (UIDAI), which runs the Aadhar programme.

Unlike Jain who was not at all forthcoming, 44-year-old Prodyut Bora, founder of the BJP's IT cell in 2007 (barely a year after Facebook and Twitter had been launched) was far from reticent while speaking to us. He had resigned from the party's national executive in February 2015 after questioning Modi and Amit Shah's "highly individualised and centralised style of decision-making" that had led to the "subversion of democratic traditions" in the government and in the party.

Bora recalled how he was one of the first graduates from the leading business school, the Indian Institute of Management, Ahmedabad, to join the BJP because of his great admiration for the then Prime Minister Atal Behari Vajpayee. It was at the behest of the then party president Rajnath Singh (who is now Union Home Minister) that he set up the party's IT cell to enable its leaders to come closer to, and interact with, their supporters. The cell, he told us, was created not with a mandate to abuse people on social media platforms. He lamented that "madness" has now gripped the BJP and the desire to win elections at any cost has "destroyed the very ethos" of the party he was once a part of. Today, the Gurgaon-based Bora runs a firm making air purification equipment and is involved with an independent political party in his home state, Assam.

He told us: "The process of being economical with the truth (in the BJP) began in 2014. The (election) campaign was sending out unverified facts, infomercials, memes, dodgy data and graphs. From there, fake news was one step up the curve. Leaders of political parties, including the BJP, like to outsource this work because they don't want to leave behind digital footprints. In 2009, social media platforms like Facebook and WhatsApp had a marginal impact in India's 20 big cities. By 2014, however, it had virtually replaced the traditional mass media. In 2019, it will be the most pervasive media in the country."

Bora is of the view that social media will "play a perverse role" in the 2019 general elections. He went to the extent of comparing the BJP's IT cell with SIMI or the Students' Islamic Movement of India, which has been banned by the government for its extremist character. At the same time, the founder of the BJP's IT cell sees a silver lining in the dark clouds of disinformation that pervades the country's social media. "Residents in these 20 big cities are now growing suspicious of social media," he said, adding: "They no longer blindly trust everything that is put out on WhatsApp."

Bora had left the IT cell and moved to Assam to work for the BJP by the time Nitin Gadkari replaced Rajnath Singh as BJP president. A Mumbai-based IT specialist, who is close to Gadkari, then played an important role in helping the party organise its internet and social media strategies. He was Vinit Goenka (briefly quoted earlier). Like Bora, he was loquacious in telling us how the party used Facebook and WhatsApp to spread the BJP's agenda and boost Modi's image.

Unlike Bora, however, Goenka remains firmly aligned with the party and particularly with his political mentor. He is a member of a task force on IT in the Ministry of Shipping and the Ministry of Road Transport and Highways, both headed by Gadkari. Goenka is also a member of the governing council of the Centre for Railway Information System (CRIS) in the Ministry of Railways headed by Piyush Goyal.

At one stage in our interview with Goenka that lasted over two hours, we asked him a pointed question: "Who helped whom more, Facebook or the BJP?"

He smiled and said: "That's a difficult question. I wonder whether the BJP helped Facebook more than Facebook helped the BJP. You could say, we helped each other."

Having been a member of the party's youth wing since 2003, with Gadkari's prodding, Goenka joined the BJP's IT cell in Maharashtra in 2008 to help "modernise" the party. His first successful initiative was to supervise the setting up of high-definition video conferencing facilities in different districts of the state to enable leaders like Gadkari to interact regularly with the BJP's *karyakarta*s (or party personnel). He did not look back thereafter and rapidly expanded his operations across the country. By the time election campaigning started picking up in late-2013, he had put together a network of over 78,000 people who were fully engaged in aggressively promoting the interests of Modi and the BJP in rural blocks and urban wards in 29 states and seven Union Territories. Significantly, in each group, one person was deputed to focus on the social media, Facebook, WhatsApp and Twitter.

Goenka also played a key role in connecting BJP's leaders with IT industry bigwigs, including Som Mittal and Rajendra Pawar and business associations like the Indo–US Business Council. He helped his party organise regular meetings with IT professionals and entrepreneurs. The meetings were called "Let's Talk Governance" and held every Saturday at the BJP's office at 11 Ashoka Road in central Delhi.

Speaking to us in his office in south Delhi, he recalled: "In 2012, the liberal media fiefdom broke with (the rise of the) social media. Politicians started interacting directly with their constituents. The period between 2012 and 2014 was a period when the Congress government was being exposed for corruption. (People's) trust in the government and the media was falling... We started reacting to the media and started writing on the internet. Everyone was empowered. But we used... (the social media) better than others."

Forty-six-year-old Goenka, who used to work with IBM and belongs to a Mumbai-based family that has been traditional supporters of the RSS, told us: "We made a network of NRIs (non-resident Indians) in the US and asked each one of them to call their contacts in India to participate in online activities including live chats, liking pages and participating in online groups on Facebook and WhatsApp."

8

Promoting a Messiah

By 2013, Shivnath Thukral had entered the picture to become an important player in the online campaign to promote Modi and the BJP. Thukral had left *New Delhi Television (NDTV)* in October 2009 as an anchor of television programmes on the corporate sector and stock-markets to join the Essar group (promoted by the Ruia family) as its group president, corporate branding and strategic initiatives. The Essar group had supported various events and festivals, including the "Think" festival hosted by *Tehelka* magazine in Goa. His wife Shaili Chopra (another television journalist and anchor) was subsequently employed by the magazine. More about Chopra and her venture *SheThePeople* a little later.

An aside: *The Essar group, which has interests in oil, gas, steel and power, has had more than its share of controversies in recent times, some of them on account of the huge debt burden of particular group companies. The names of some of its promoters and their relatives cropped up in the scandal relating to allotment of second-generation (2G) telecommunications spectrum. In 2015, a whistle-blower leaked internal information about the group, which, among other things,*

revealed that gifts of expensive mobile phones and other facilities –
hospitality and transport – had been made available to important
politicians, bureaucrats and journalists. There have been media reports,
including in The Caravan, *that the Essar group had provided jobs*
to persons recommended by politicians, including former President of
India Pranab Mukherjee. Gadkari reportedly availed of hospitality
from the Essar group in France.

Thukral went on to join the Carnegie Foundation in
India and thereafter, became director of policy for India and
South Asia for Facebook in India as an important executive
interfacing with government bureaucrats, technocrats and
politicians together with Ankhi Das. In the run-up to the
2014 elections, from late-2013 onwards, Thukral, along with
investment banker, Anuj Gupta, helped Hiren Joshi create and
run *Mera Bharosa* (literally translated to mean "My Trust") and
other web pages for the party. He had become an unofficial
member of the BJP's social media team.

It was difficult for us to access the pages that *Mera Bharosa*
had put out before the 2014 elections. We were assisted by
researcher Nishant Saxena to retrieve some of these pages
from websites that archive content on the internet that has
subsequently been removed or redacted. A look through these
pages reveals a plethora of propaganda, all directed against
the Congress, then led by Sonia Gandhi and the United
Progressive Alliance (UPA) government headed by Manmohan
Singh. Much of the content in these pages, including graphics,
images and cartoons, is disinformation with a single purpose:
to build Modi's image as a mythical strong leader and trash
his political opponents, notably those belonging to the Indian
National Congress.

Here are a few illustrative examples of headlines of articles from October 2013 that were put up on the website: "How Sonia Gandhi pumps up onion prices," "Sonia Gandhi makes India worse than Africa" and "Impotent Congress." In November that year, Anuj Gupta himself wrote an article for *Mera Bharosa* titled "Modi and Licence Raj: Licence to Liberty" raising expectations of new liberalised economic policies if Modi was elected to power. Gupta was then working with a consultancy outfit called Strategic Decisions Group with offices in Hong Kong and Mumbai that hired managers with Masters of Business Administration (MBA) degrees/diplomas from reputed educational institutions like the Indian Institutes of Management (IIMs) and engineers from the Indian Institutes of Technology (IITs).

A person who had sought a job with *Mera Bharosa* said he had come across Gupta at the June 2013 launch in Mumbai of the website of a right-wing organisation called *Subhodini* which is a platform engaged in dissemination of information on Indian history and Indic culture. This person was later interviewed for the job by Gupta and Thukral.

Prodyut Bora was of the view that "a semi-political activist (like Thukral) joining (what is supposed to be) a neutral platform raises serious concerns." A member of the Congress, who spoke to us on condition of anonymity, said Thukral's involvement in Modi's pre-election campaign and subsequently, his frequent meetings with Dr Hiren Joshi, made him wonder if Facebook would be truly unbiased during the election campaigns leading up to the 2019 elections. Another IT industry professional, who too spoke off-the-record, had a different opinion and said Thukral had appeared to him to be politically non-aligned. "I guess he is just acting at the behest of his employer and his colleagues," he speculated.

Facebook's official spokesperson chose not to respond to our specific questions on Shivnath Thukral's activities before he was recruited by the organization. She stated: "Our goal is to hire the best people for the roles available, not just in India, but also globally. And this was the process followed for Shivnath's hiring."

Mera Bharosa was not the only web initiative of its kind before the 2014 elections. Others included *Kamal Sandesh* (Information from the Lotus – the BJP's election symbol), *Mere Sapnon Ka Bharat* (India of My Dreams), *True Indian* and *Centre Right* run by Prasanna Viswanathan, the current CEO of the right-wing website and magazine *Swarajya* (meaning self-rule, a word/phrase used frequently during India's anti-colonial movement).

"Narendra Modi's campaign began with positive content about the so-called Gujarat model of development and then went on to criticise the Congress party," says Pratik Sinha, editor of the fact-checking website, *AltNews*. "It was after coming to power in May 2014 that they (supporters of the BJP) started seeding disinformation – intentionally manipulated information – and unleashing trolls on the critics of the government and the party. This went out of control and became a problem after 2016."

He pointed out that the BJP's supporters were among the earliest adopters and users of social media platforms like Facebook, WhatsApp and Twitter. But they were fragmented across geographies, time zones and platforms. It was the Modi campaign that brought them all together in a centralised fashion. "The 150-odd trolls Modi met in July 2015 had been lurking on these platforms and seeding problematic information for the campaign well before the party came to power," Sinha said.

Before the 2014 elections, the BJP was Facebook's only major political client in India. Ankhi Das worked closely with Joshi and made regular visits to Modi's office in Gandhinagar. The relationship between Facebook and the Modi campaign grew deeper following his electoral victory in May 2014. Two days after the election results were announced, Das wrote a gushing op-ed article in *Quartz India* about Facebook's role in Modi's victory.[3]

Another article by her was published nearly two years later in March 2017 and is available on Prime Minister Modi's personal website. It is titled "Prime Minister Modi and the new art of public governance." She is described here as the director for public policy for Facebook in India, South Asia and Central Asia, and mentions that she has over 17 years of experience in public policy and regulatory affairs in the technology sector. At the end of the article is the usual disclaimer: "The views expressed above belong to the author(s) and the Narendra Modi website and Narendra Modi App does not necessarily endorse the views expressed."

Earlier, in 2015, the Modi government rallied support for the social media platform by announcing an e-governance scheme called "Digital India" – all government ministries and

---

3   https://qz.com/210639/how-likes-bring-votes-narendra-modis-campaign-on-facebook/.

departments, ministers and bureaucrats were asked to create Facebook pages to reach out to their friends and constituents. In effect, Facebook became the default communication platform for the government of India. In the years that followed, supporters of the BJP started "weaponising" Facebook, Instagram and WhatsApp to target voices critical of Modi and his party.

These three social media platforms together comprise the biggest advertising network of its kind in the history of humankind. These have huge design issues that go beyond leaking user data. Facebook and its sister platforms are not just addictive but seek to convert politics into games. Democracy, access to information and interpersonal interactions turn into games of engagement: likes, shares, comments and a race to gather more followers.

In India, representatives of various political parties have been reported stating that the chances of a person getting a party ticket to stand for elections would go up if the concerned person had a large number of followers on Facebook. In March 2018, Prime Minister Modi asked his party MPs how many of them had over 300,000 "genuine likes" on their Facebook pages and said he would incentivise such MPs by appearing on video conferences for their supporters.

The social media giant is no ordinary corporate conglomerate. As *The New York Times (NYT)* recently put it: "In just over a decade, Facebook has connected more than 2.2 billion people, a global nation unto itself that reshaped political campaigns, the advertising business and daily life around the world. Along the way, Facebook accumulated one of the largest-ever repositories of personal data, a treasure trove of photos, messages and likes that propelled the company into the Fortune 500 (list of the world's largest companies)."

Facebook makes money, and lots and lots of it, on engagement. "Commercial, political and personal speech are different – Facebook short-circuits democracy by blurring the lines between and among them," said Dr Ravi Sundaram, media scholar at the "Sarai" programme of the Centre for the Study of Developing Societies, a Delhi-based think-tank, adding: "It is an infrastructure that makes money by conflating all forms of messaging and speech into commercial speech."

Facebook, WhatsApp and Instagram, together also comprise the biggest consciousness manipulation infrastructure of its kind that has been constructed on a scale never seen before in the history of humankind. In 2012, Facebook conducted a notorious global experiment to evaluate how changes to its news feeds affected the emotional state of its users. The results published in 2014 were not surprising. When users see more positive content on their feeds, they post positive content. And when people see negative posts, they post negative things.

Simple, but true! Facebook makes lots and lots of money by manipulating the consciousness of its unsuspecting users. Extreme content generates extreme emotions and, therefore, increases engagement. Advertisers realised this quite quickly. The tactics employed by political hackers are borrowed from the playbook of advertisers. Facebook does its part by providing support to political operatives to generate better, more effective and more polarising messaging.

In this book, we have already examined the role played by Facebook and WhatsApp in disseminating fake news, hate speech and incendiary information and their alleged complicity with Modi and the BJP. We have reported on how Facebook arrived at the dominant position it is in India at present with more than a little help from the current ruling regime. We continue to outline the role played by key individuals with close links with the BJP and Prime Minister Modi in propagating his party's right-wing Hindu nationalist agenda on social media platforms like Facebook.

9

Converting Politics into Games

It was in the second week of October 2018 that a meeting took place between an influential Congress Member of Parliament, a few party functionaries handling the party's social media campaigns and Ankhi Das, Facebook's senior representative in India. We were told by a reliable source that during the meeting, Das was asked why Facebook had refused permission to the Congress to place paid-for advertisements on its platform that would propagate the opposition party's claims on, among other issues, the Rafale fighter aircraft deal. Das reportedly said that she was unaware about what had happened and would look into the complaint.

When we sent an email to Divya Spandana, who handles the Congress party's social media campaigns, to confirm whether our facts were correct or not, she promptly responded by saying the information we had received was "not true at all." We also asked her if she would like to inform us about when the Congress had started working with Facebook and whether the organisation had conducted workshops and/or provided onsite support to representatives of her party. She did not respond to these queries.

We sent a similar email to the spokesperson of Facebook in New Delhi and received a different kind of response. This is what was stated:

> (On the) Congress and advertising, we went back to them on guidelines and clarifications when setting up advertising. Their advertisements ran into scheduling issues for several reasons:
>
> a.   The time limit they set for advertising; they have to seek approvals for content and policies, they ran out of the time for scheduling ads before the approvals came, hence the ad could not run.
>
> b.   They have been guided to set enough scheduling time before the ads run.
>
> c.   We did a deep dive and they have had several ads run on the platform, so it would be unfair to say that Facebook did not guarantee approvals to run ads.
>
> You can get more details on our advertising approval process here:
>
> https://www.facebook.com/policies/ads/.

In October 2017, a bill was introduced in the United States Senate to enact the "Honest Ads Act" to promote regulation of political advertising online by companies like Facebook and Google. In the US, media organisations are legally mandated by the Federal Election Campaign Act of 1971 to disclose who has paid how much for political advertisements on television, print publications and on radio channels. However, these requirements do not apply to web platforms. The bill seeks to amend the 1971 law to make digital platforms disclose the source of funds and the names of persons/entities who purchase time and space for political advertisements and also to ensure that "reasonable efforts" are made so that the ads are not purchased "directly or indirectly" by individuals and organisations located in foreign countries.

On 30 October, *VICE News* in the US reported that the "paid for by" disclosure at the top of each political advertisement on Facebook, ostensibly to bring about greater transparency, could be "easily manipulated." The media organisation applied to buy fake advertisements on behalf of 100 sitting US Senators and found that all of these were "promptly approved" by Facebook.

Parminder Singh, executive director of IT for Change, a non-government organisation, pointed out that Facebook agreed to abide by the Honest Ads Act even before it was enacted in the US. He asked: "Will it follow similar standards for India?"

The company's critics have contended that what Facebook has agreed to comply with in the US is a diluted version of what has been proposed in the amendment to the Federal Election Campaign Act in order to pre-empt tougher regulations.

In 2015 and 2016, a team of journalists from an internationally-renowned publication based in the US led by an award-winning journalist had started an investigation into the activities of Facebook in India. One of the areas that was sought to be probed was the alleged mismatch in the posts and pages taken down by Facebook in comparison to those taken down after following orders issued by the Indian government's Computer Emergency Response Team (CERT) in the Ministry (earlier Department) of Electronics and Information Technology (MEITY/DEITY) and other ministries and departments. The investigation was never completed and the award-winning journalist moved back from India to the US. Our pointed questions to Facebook on allegations of discrepancies in the data put out by the organisation in comparison to MEITY did not elicit a direct answer.

The transparency report released by Facebook on 16 November shows a consistent increase in the number of government requests for "information" and details of "user accounts," usually by law enforcement agencies, over the last five years. Information requests have jumped more than five-fold from 3,245 in the first half of calendar 2013 to 16,580 in the January–June period in 2018. In these periods, the number of requests for details of user accounts have gone up over 5.5 times from 4,144 to 23,047. India is now second after the US in terms of numbers of both types of requests for information.

Between the first halves of 2015 and 2018, while there has been an estimated increase in Facebook accounts in India by 63 per cent, the number of information requests by government agencies has shot up almost three-fold. The increase between January–June 2017 and the corresponding period in 2018 was more than 67 per cent. In 2013, India was on top of the list of countries in terms of requests for content take-down but is now down to the seventh position – the lowest thus far since Facebook started compiling and disclosing such data.

Facebook says it complied with the Indian government's requests roughly half the time. Interestingly, in terms of compliance, India's position has collapsed, from being in the top 20 (out of 71 countries) to 70th position (out of 127 countries) in 2018. Equally significantly, the number of actual "take-downs" of content that had peaked in 2015 at around 30,000 is now down to below 3,500 – implying that during the period when the proliferation of disinformation is supposed to have peaked in India, Facebook took down problematic content at a slower pace.

Predictably the bulk of the content take-down requests from the government have related to religious sentiments, hate speech and, not surprisingly, "anti-state defamation."[4]

---

4 The full report can be accessed at: https://transparency.facebook.com/government-data-requests.

10

Cambridge Analytica in India

The reputation of Facebook took a big beating across the world in March 2018 after it was revealed that a political consultancy outfit called Cambridge Analytica – run by a UK-based company named Strategic Communications Laboratories (SCL) led by Alexander Nix – had illegally harvested personal data of over 87 million users of Facebook, most of them located in the US. Of this huge number, only a small proportion – around 562,000 – were apparently users based in India.

On 24 November 2018, UK-based *The Guardian* reported that the British Parliament had used its legal powers to seize internal documents of Facebook in an "extraordinary" attempt to hold the social media giant to account after Mark Zuckerberg repeatedly refused to answer questions raised by MPs. The publication claimed that the cache of confidential documents contained "significant revelations" about Facebook's "decisions on data and privacy controls that led to the Cambridge Analytica scandal." These documents were obtained by invoking a "rare Parliamentary mechanism" to compel the founder of an American software company called Six4Three to disclose information. A Facebook spokesperson said this company's claims had "no merit" and that the disclosure of the documents would violate an order of a court in California, US.

Prabir Purkayastha, who heads the *NewsClick* portal (which published the series of articles we wrote) and who has been opposing digital monopolies, told us: "What Cambridge Analytica could do when it illegally misused data from users of Facebook to manipulate political preferences, Facebook can theoretically do the same much better, more effectively and more subtly in-house. It can deploy 'soft' promotion or demotion of content and pages more effectively internally – and do this deeper, wider and faster."

Despite the relatively small number of users involved in this country, the Cambridge Analytica scandal led to a big political slanging match in India with leaders of both the BJP and the Congress accusing each other of having used the services of an associate company of Cambridge Analytica in India, namely, Strategic Communications Laboratories. This company had four directors, two from the UK including Nix and two from India, Amrish Kumar Tyagi, and Avneesh Kumar Rai. The company had been active through another associate firm, Ovleno Business Intelligence, headed by Tyagi – who is the son of K C Tyagi, leader of the Janata Dal (United) which is the ruling party in Bihar – together with Himanshu Sharma, who worked on Modi's "Mission 272+" campaign and the BJP's "missed call" campaign.

There were other firms associated with Tyagi and Rai that have escaped media attention, which we are disclosing here. These companies include the Lucknow-based Stealth Analytics and Business Solutions Private Limited, Routier Operations Consulting Private Limited, Span House Customer Services Private Limited. Among those associated with these firms were graduates of the Indian Institute of Management, Lucknow. The names of some of the individuals associated with these corporate entities were Ankur Dahiya, Adwait Vikram Singh, Maddela Giri Kumar.[5] Cambridge Analytica claimed that it worked with the JD(U)–BJP alliance in the run-up to the 2010 Bihar assembly elections. On its now-suspended website, it had contended: "Our client achieved a landslide victory, with over 90 per cent of total seats targeted by CA being won."

In an interview in *The Print* news portal on 27 March, Rai said he had worked as an election adviser for various political parties since 1984. Before the 2009 Lok Sabha

---

5   Details of some of these companies and persons can be accessed using the following links:

https://www.tofler.in/visualization?cin=U93000DL2007PTC 169445

https://www.tofler.in/amrish-kumar-tyagi/director/01270318

https://www.tofler.in/avneesh-kumar-rai/director/02964979

https://www.tofler.in/stealth-analytics-and-business-solutions-private-limited/company/U74999UP2017PTC094815

https://www.tofler.in/ankur-dahiya/director/07797248

https://www.linkedin.com/in/ankur-dahiya-104891102/

https://www.linkedin.com/in/girikumarmaddela/

https://www.tofler.in/routier-operations-consulting-private-limited/company/U60300HR2018PTC072834

https://www.tofler.in/visualization?cin=U93000DL2007PTC 169445 elections, Rai worked with BJP leader from Noida (Gautam Buddh Nagar) in Uttar Pradesh Mahesh Sharma, who is Union Culture Minister in the Modi government. Rai's friend and professional associate Tyagi had worked on gathering business intelligence besides data that would be of use to politicians and political parties. The two reportedly compiled databases of households in states with details of their caste affiliation and political preferences that could be used by candidates standing for elections. According to Rai, a team from Cambridge Analytica met representatives of both the BJP and the Congress to seek business opportunities and pitched for work relating to the assembly elections in Rajasthan and Madhya Pradesh. He alleged that Nix had "double-crossed" or "two-timed" his clients to earn as much as money as he could.

In March 2018, a day after testifying before a British Parliamentary Committee, Christopher Wylie, who blew the whistle on Cambridge Analytica's activities, claimed that its projects in India were akin to "modern colonialism" and that the company had data from hundreds of thousands of villages in all districts in India. He released data suggesting that Cambridge Analytica and its associates had worked since 2003 during the campaigns before assembly elections that had taken place in Uttar Pradesh, Bihar, Kerala, West Bengal, Assam, Jharkhand, Madhya Pradesh and Rajasthan and also before the general elections of 2009 where "proprietary data collection methodologies" were used by "a number of Lok Sabha candidates" for campaigning strategies.

The Wire portal reported that Avneesh Kumar Rai flatly denied Wylie's claims.

While representatives of Cambridge Analytica and its

associates had met individuals connected with both the BJP and the Congress, party functionaries denied having engaged them for professional services. In this context, in an interview published in the *Hindustan Times* on 30 March, Praveen Chakravarty who heads the Congress party's data analytics department, sought to differentiate between public data and private data on social media. He said: "Whatever a Twitter user posts is for (the) public. But if a Facebook user puts something out only for friends and not for (the) public, I cannot use that. So, we have to have this distinction clearly separated. I think it is very clear that anything that crosses the boundary of public to private without the consent of the individual is breach of privacy."

Chakravarty went on to quip: "There was... a breach of trust by Facebook... This breach is the fundamental problem. And this issue is as much about Facebook as it is about Cambridge Analytica. In the context of a recent India example, if Cambridge Analytica is Nirav Modi, Facebook is the Punjab National Bank. That is the breach. Both are culprits." (In February 2018, Nirav Modi and his associates were accused of defrauding India's second largest bank to the extent of nearly ₹13,000 crore or around $1.8 million.)

Chakravarty's analogies and comparisons can be controverted. Every bit of information that is put out in Facebook or Twitter is "public" with the exception of specific kinds of "private messages" and information about the personal details of users that are provided during the time such users register themselves on these social media platforms. Arguably all other data is "derived" by Facebook and other social media platforms, including information on users' political preferences not to mention their possible sexual orientation, financial status, emotional states and so on.

The Indian government sent show-cause notices to Cambridge Analytica on 23 March 2018 and to Facebook on 28 March. "What security architecture is proposed to be created by Facebook, on an urgent basis, so that the data concerning Indians is not pilfered or manipulated again for extraneous purposes including to influence the elections," the government asked Facebook in its notice.

Other questions asked by the government were:

- whether the personal data of Indian voters had been "compromised" by Cambridge Analytica or "any other downstream entity in any manner,"
- whether Facebook or its related or downstream agencies utilising its data had earlier been engaged to "manipulate the Indian electoral process" and if "any such downstream entity misused data from Facebook," and
- what is the "protection available to the data subject." Cambridge Analytica claimed that it had collected data in India only from "first party research instruments or opinion surveys" and did not hold data of Indian users obtained illegally from Facebook.

On 26 July, Union Minister for Electronics and Information Technology Ravi Shankar Prasad had told the Parliament that the Central Bureau of Investigation had been asked to probe Cambridge Analytica's misuse of data of Facebook users in India. Meanwhile, in Menlo Park, California, Facebook's bosses reportedly rued that its profits would decline for "several years" due to the company having to incur higher costs on improving privacy standards.

★ ★ ★

In the wake of the Cambridge Analytica scandal, there was quite a churn in the higher echelons of Facebook and entities related to it. In September 2018, Brian Acton and Jan Koum, co-founders of WhatsApp, left the board of the parent company following "philosophical misalignments" with Zuckerberg and Sandberg. Acton later said he was unhappy that WhatsApp would no longer be free of "advertisements, games and gimmicks" as had been envisaged by him. He had "sacrificed" monetisation of content but this was clearly not what Zuckerberg wanted. Moreover, he was clear he did not want to sell the privacy of users.

"Private greed militates against privacy," observed Purkayastha.

The same month, Instagram's founders Kevin Systrom and Mike Krieger also left Facebook amid speculation that they were first unhappy and then agitated over Zuckerberg's alleged meddling. Unlike Acton, however, they did not openly criticize Zuckerberg.

Across the world there has been an outpouring of criticism against Facebook in recent months. *Bloomberg* had reported in December 2017 that Elizabeth Linder, who started and ran Facebook's political accounts in Europe, Middle East and Africa accounts till 2016, left the company because she grew uncomfortable with what she saw as an increased emphasis on electioneering and political campaigns.

A day after the United Nations ordered an independent investigation into Facebook's role in the genocide of Rohingyas in Myanmar, the company put out a public statement admitting that "it was too slow" to address hate speech in that country and had banned pages run by the Myanmar military junta much later than it should have. By the time Facebook reacted, nearly 700,000 Rohingyas were reportedly displaced from their homes in one of the worst genocides of its kind in recent times.

In Sri Lanka, civil society groups had been producing evidence and warning Facebook for months that its inaction on hate speech would lead to violence. The company finally acted after the Sri Lankan government banned the organisation accusing it of fuelling violence against Muslims that led to several incidents of arson and the deaths of three persons. In Germany, Facebook assisted the anti-immigrant party Alternative for Germany or AfD.

In Philippines, Facebook reportedly helped train campaign managers of Rodrigo Duterte who encouraged extra-judicial killings and allegedly continues to use the social media platform to silence his critics and political opponents. In some South Asian countries, including Philippines, the number of users on Facebook grew exponentially after using its Free Basics scheme. Independent research suggests that many users in these countries conflate Facebook with the internet. Facebook and its associated platforms have been linked to violence across countries in South Asia, including India, besides Libya and Germany.

Before the recently-concluded elections in Brazil, it was revealed by the newspaper *Folha de S.Paulo* that private companies linked to President Jair Bolsonaro had flooded WhatsApp groups and Facebook with disinformation and inflammatory content. Paid activists and digital agencies were hired to seed content on these platforms. A day after this investigative report was published, WhatsApp and Facebook placed restrictions on their platforms and "de-platformed" thousands of users, including Bolsonaro's son. However, some of these restrictions were circumvented by using subscriber identity modules (SIMs) and accounts that were located outside Brazil.

In Cambodia, opposition parties have demanded a probe into incumbent President Hun Sen's online influence campaign after the local media investigated and found that the president was buying "likes" and "shares" on the social media from India-based content marketing companies.

One of our sources told us that while many have argued that companies based in China that are operating in India pose threats to this country's national security, it can be argued that a bigger threat to the integrity of elections and democratic institutions here is the way certain digital marketing companies are operating. In India, as in Brazil, supporters of political parties are reportedly using SIMs registered in foreign countries to bypass restrictions.

On 17 May 2018, Facebook announced a partnership with the Washington-based Atlantic Council and Digital Forensic Research Laboratory (DFRL) to "independently monitor disinformation and other vulnerabilities in elections globally, including in India" so that the Laboratory can become its "eyes and ears" to spot potential abuse. Since then, DFRL has produced multiple reports on India. The most recent report on Twitter reads: " while bots were used on both sides on February 9-10 [2019], the pro Modi traffic was for more heavily manipulated than the anti Modi traffic, and indeed far more heavily manipulated than any large-scale traffic flow the DFRL has analysed of yet."

11

Influencing Politics

Katie Harbath, Facebook's global politics and government outreach director, in an interview published by *The Economic Times* on 13 August, said her organisation was doubling the size of its team of reviewers globally from 10,000 to 20,000 to scan accounts and remove fake ones. It has teamed up with, among others, *BOOMLive*, a fact-checking website.

Chris Daniels of WhatsApp told *ET* that it was one of the few technology companies to intentionally constrain sharing. He said his company would be investing more in identifying and banning automated accounts using machine-learning classifiers to analyse accounts for automated or abnormal behaviour and spam. After issuing a call for applications in July and receiving more than 600 proposals, on 12 November, WhatsApp announced awards for 20 research teams across the world, including India, to contribute to its "understanding of how misinformation spreads." Each grant would be around $50,000 or around ₹36 lakh.

Much of the focus of Facebook's management in controlling damage to its reputation has been in the US and in Europe where it faces regulatory challenges. In the US, the company has taken steps such as archiving political advertisements and making these public; been more proactive in taking down posts that apparently seek to influence voter behaviour; made more information on groups and pages public, and; purged fake accounts as well as pages and groups disseminating information considered problematic. By way of comparison, in South Asia and in India, Facebook seems to have acted in a cavalier and even callous manner, until recently. In India, as in other developing countries, Facebook has evidently sought to treat disinformation as more of a public relations problem.

Across the world, there is growing awareness of how Facebook has often succeeded in making politics appear akin to a game and, in the process, disrupted and weakened systems and institutions responsible for strengthening democracy and provided authoritarian rulers opportunities to manipulate electoral processes. Disinformation is the cheapest tool in the hand of such rulers and Facebook has often looked the other way till a stink has been raised.

In the US, investigations have been conducted on whether the infrastructure of the digital giant was misused to manipulate the 2016 elections by financially strong and ideologically motivated individuals and groups. Independent digital forensic organisations and the media continue to uncover circumstantial evidence of how the US elections were allegedly sought to be influenced using Facebook's platforms. Reports have appeared suggesting that Facebook was aware of how its platforms could have been manipulated – through internal communications put out in 2016 itself by Alex Stamos, the organisation's former chief security officer. However, the organisation did not acknowledge this till much later. Stamos left Facebook in August 2018. His position remains vacant and his team has been assigned different duties in the organisation.

As has been detailed earlier, Facebook worked closely with Modi well before he became Prime Minister of India; provided his party and his supporters support; helped make Modi the most "liked" leader on its platforms; allegedly turned a blind eye to coordinated disinformation campaigns, including against those belonging to minority communities, which led to incidents of mob lynching, besides targeting particular individual journalists and politicians who were perceived to be opposed to the ruling regime.

Facebook has conducted workshops for the BJP to use its platforms better. As information about its association with the BJP and its supporters became public, Facebook went on a public relations overdrive across India. In 2018 the company issued prominent advertisements in newspapers, conducted roadshows, sponsored events and festivals, loudly announced its partnerships with fact-checking organisations and educational institutions that teach and train aspiring journalists and media professionals and conducted training programmes for government officials.

Among the events financially supported by Facebook are ones conducted by *SheThePeople*, promoted and anchored by Shaili Chopra, who is married to Shivnath Thukral, director of policy for India and South Asia for Facebook in India, and like him used to be a television anchor for *NDTV*. A person who participated in a particular programme of *SheThePeople*

said that during a discussion on the proliferation of fake news, this person got an impression that there were not-so-subtle attempts to "shoot the messenger rather than shoot the platform." A number of individuals, including a former senior employee of Facebook in India, told us that the organisation's support to Chopra's venture was a clear case of "conflict of interest."

A spokesperson of Facebook responded to our question on this topic by stating that Facebook's association with *SheThePeople* preceded Thukral joining the organisation.

Together with Suman Chopra and his wife, Thukral is a director in Digitalist Tech Media Private Limited which owns the *SheThePeople* brand. He was, incidentally, also an additional director in Opalina Technologies Private Limited which designed the Narendra Modi's website.

We were informed by a reliable source that during a recent "informal interaction over dinner" in Washington DC, USA, Katie Harbath, global politics and government outreach director of Facebook, had remarked that she was "unhappy and uneasy about the proximity" of top officials of Facebook in India to representatives of the government of India headed by Prime Minister Modi as well as important functionaries of the ruling BJP.

We sent her an email asking her if this information was correct and also asked her to apprise us of the role she played in selecting Ankhi Das and Shivnath Thukral to important positions in Facebook in India. She promptly directed us to the spokesperson of Facebook in India who responded that over and above what had by then already been sent to us on the structure of Facebook's policy team in India and the organisation's hiring and compliance policies, "there is nothing new that Katie can add on."

In India, Facebook is attempting to change its image as a platform that is neutral and does not overtly favour the BJP. For Prime Minister Modi, social media remains an extremely important tool of communication and for political campaigning. He deeply detests a large section of the mainstream media, especially the section that had in the past highlighted his alleged complicity in the 2002 Hindu–Muslim riots in Gujarat. He is the first prime minister of India not to have addressed a "free for all" or unscripted media conference since he came to power in May 2014. He continues to prefer pre-scripted public addresses and grants interviews only to "friendly" journalists.

To quickly recapitulate, before the elections, Facebook helped Modi and his party members effectively use its platforms to fine-tune their messaging and provide feedback on what worked and what did not. Over the next few years, social media became a "weapon" and one of the biggest online disinformation ecosystems of its kind in the world. Many non-resident Indians, who are among Modi's most loyal supporters, continue to create pages, develop groups of fans and enhance his image to make him into some sort of a mythological God-like figure. At the same time, his opponents have had false information spread about them, been mercilessly trolled and satirised. Before the 2014 elections, the BJP was way ahead of others in using the social media but today, some of the party's rivals are seeking to deploy the same methods against the ruling party.

Facebook and its platforms have also made what some would consider "cosmetic" technical changes by trying to reduce the speed of contagion on WhatsApp by limiting the number of recipients a message can be forwarded to in a single click and by tagging forwarded messages. These restraints can, however, be overcome by technical experts not just by hacking but also by using third-party software to circumvent the default limits of these platforms, for example, by employing software to create multiple groups each with 256 users, the limit imposed by WhatsApp on the size of a group.

On 3 November, the British Broadcasting Corporation (BBC) reported that hackers gained access to private information of nearly 120 million Facebook users and published messages from 81,000 accounts in an effort to sell the data to earn money. The going "rate" was reportedly 10 British cents per account.

Facebook had also hired more content moderators in India – despite its constant refrain that artificial intelligence can solve most of problems arising out of the spread of disinformation on its platforms – through its third-party contractor, Genpact, operating out of Hyderabad and Bengaluru.

How effective these steps will be remains to be seen. There is every indication that India will remain the world's biggest hate-creating factory on social media. The digital fingerprints of India have been found across political conversations in South Africa, the Philippines, Cambodia, Brazil and Mexico. Numerous India-based public relations, campaign-management and digital marketing companies regularly employ "bot networks" and "sock-puppet accounts" to impact social media conversations in countries across the planet.

Among such companies is CNet Infosystems, based out of Noida in Uttar Pradesh, which allegedly tried to "game" political conversations in South Africa on behalf of the discredited Gupta brothers who were accused of corruption and trying to buy political influence in that country when Jacob Zuma was in power. The company, with the help of the disgraced public relations behemoth Bell Pottinger, allegedly set up numerous disinformation websites and bot-networks on Twitter and Facebook to advance the cause of some of the Gupta brothers who are now reportedly absconding.

Fire Eye, a cybersecurity firm, released a report in 2018 which claimed that Indian currency was used to buy problematic advertisements on Facebook before and after the 2016 Presidential elections in the US. The involvement of Indian public relations and digital marketing companies is also suspected in the recently-concluded elections in Mexico and Brazil, according to investigations by the Digital Forensics Research Laboratory.

An investigation by *AltNews* exposed one of the companies that is allegedly spreading disinformation on Facebook, namely, a firm named Silver Touch Technologies. Incidentally, one of the biggest clients of this firm is the government of India! More about Silver Touch will be found later in this book.

Besides Silver Touch, other digital companies like Fourth Dimension and TSD Corps have been in the past been linked to the BJP and the Modi government. Software that can create huge WhatsApp broadcast groups, link WhatsApp numbers to Facebook accounts and create databases of WhatsApp numbers linked to electoral data at the booth level are available in the market for as little as ₹500.

That social media is being increasingly used and misused

to influence and manipulate political preferences of voters in the April–May 2019 general elections, is evident to all. On 12 November 2018, the BBC released detailed research findings that clearly indicated that a "rising tide of nationalism in India is driving ordinary citizens to spread fake news" and that "facts were less important to some than the emotional desire to bolster national identity" – these findings may sound like music to the ears to certain supporters of Modi. Like Trump, India's Prime Minister is a demagogue who seeks political support by appealing to emotions that are often divorced from facts and factual analysis.

The day its research findings were made public, the BBC organised a discussion on fake news at the Indian Institute of Technology, Delhi, where representatives of Facebook, Google and Twitter defended their efforts to curb the spread of disinformation on their platforms before the 2019 elections, while acknowledging that there persisted contentious issues that remained unresolved. According to a report in *The Indian Express*, the moderator asked the audience (mainly comprising students and journalists): "…who here is more optimistic about trying to get to grips with this problem in terms of what the tech companies are doing?"

No one in the audience raised her or his hands.

We sought appointments with Ankhi Das and Shivnath Thukral for on-the-record interviews. We emailed a list of 64 questions that covered, among other issues, the working of Facebook's policy team in India, its relationship with Modi and the BJP, its content moderation policies, and allegations of conflict of interest in the case of Thukral. We received a response from Facebook's spokesperson in

India. Our questions and the responses we received from Facebook are reproduced verbatim. But before we do that, a little more on the crisis of credibility that Facebook is currently facing.

12

Crisis of Credibility

The biggest online social media group in the world is reeling under an unprecedented crisis of credibility. The crisis intensified following the publication on 14 November of a 5,000-word investigation by *The New York Times* alleging a host of questionable practices by Facebook, the digital conglomerate that includes WhatsApp and Instagram. Here is a paragraph from the *NYT* report that encapsulates its allegations against Mark Zuckerberg, the 34-year-old founder and chief executive officer of Facebook and his 49-year-old deputy, chief operating officer Sheryl Sandberg.

> ... as evidence accumulated that Facebook's power could also be exploited to disrupt elections, broadcast viral propaganda and inspire deadly campaigns of hate around the globe, Mr. Zuckerberg and Ms. Sandberg stumbled. Bent on growth, the pair ignored warning signs and then sought to conceal them from public view. At critical moments over the last three years, they were distracted by personal projects,

and passed off security and policy decisions to subordinates, according to current and former executives.

The *NYT* claimed that the two were aware of allegations of Russian meddling in the US Presidential elections in 2016 but chose to ignore it for months. Further, it has been stated that Facebook had engaged the services of a dodgy public relations firm with links to Republican lawmakers that had sought to trash the company's critics, including George Soros who had described Facebook as "a menace to society."

A day after the *NYT* expose, Zuckerberg dispensed with the services of this public relations firm and said he was ignorant about some of its egregious practices which included alleging that some of Facebook's critics were anti-semitic – both Zuckerberg and Sandberg are of Jewish origin. This is not the first time that Facebook's bosses have reacted to criticism in a knee-jerk manner. While the two have refuted specific allegations levelled against them, their leadership abilities and integrity have been questioned, perhaps like never before.

Investors in Facebook have called for the resignation of Zuckerberg and Sandberg. As already mentioned, the company's critics are arguing that the time is opportune for the digital monopoly to be broken up in the manner in which the Bell Group or AT&T was fragmented into competing entities in the early-1980s.

Our investigation into the activities of Facebook in India has revealed that while the international digital giant claims it provides an agnostic platform for all to use, there is definite evidence to indicate that senior employees of the organisation have in the past worked, and continue to work, very closely with Modi and the country's ruling BJP since 2011. Their proximity has been uncomfortably close leading many to wonder if Facebook will act in a neutral manner in the run-up to the general elections scheduled for April–May 2019.

★ ★ ★

Eleven years ago, in 2007, Elliot Scharge, then the vice president, global communications, Google, had talked of "e-politics" and anticipated that digital platforms would soon start micro-targeting individuals to influence their political preferences.

Jaijit Bhattacharya, president, Centre for Digital Economy Policy Research, a think-tank based in New Delhi, told us:

> In 2012, I had gone public stating that social media platforms such as Facebook would get significantly used and misused for political purposes and that this would have considerable impact on the decision-making processes of large sections of the Indian electorate. This leverage over voters would lead to these social media platforms having a disproportionately high influencing power over the government, thereby subverting the sovereignty of the nation… technologies that are invading our households which are based on artificial intelligence and speech recognition would become the next means by which the population will get finely segmented at the level of an individual thus enabling processes through which she or he can be directly influenced politically.

That Facebook's representatives have conducted workshops and training programmes for BJP functionaries and supporters as well as provided on-site support during election campaigns, is common knowledge to insiders but not so well known to the public at large. The organisation, of course, argues that it is willing to provide such services to any political party that wants them. But Facebook's association with India's ruling establishment is more pervasive and arguably, insidious as well.

Katie Harbath, the digital conglomerate's global politics and government outreach director was feted by the President of India Ram Nath Kovind in the presence of Minister for Electronics and Information Technology Ravi Shankar Prasad and the then Chief Election Commissioner O P Rawat, on 25 January 2018 for Facebook's contribution to "voter education." However, the Election Commission of India has been reticent in disclosing details of its relationship with Facebook.

Hyderabad-based media researcher Padmaja Shaw raised a number of questions under the Right to Information Act seeking information from the Election Commission of India as to the basis of, and/or the consultation process through which it entered into, joint activities with Facebook; the letters and agreements to this effect and the conditions that are binding on Facebook and on the Commission; the deliverables from Facebook and compensations if any; the precautions taken to protect privacy of citizens, and; the levels of access to information on voters. She wrote to us over email that more than six months had gone by but no response has been forthcoming to the questions she asked of the Commission. She has appealed to the Central Information Commission to ask the Election Commission of India to provide her the information she is seeking.

Facebook has struck partnerships with many media organisations in India and has provided financial, logistical and infrastructural support to them. This could be an important reason why criticism of the digital giant's activities in India have been rather muted.

What has been particularly disturbing is the manner in which Facebook's sister platform WhatsApp has been misused. Spokespersons of WhatsApp repeatedly emphasise that the "end-to-end encryption" that is "integral" to the social media platform means that even WhatsApp does not know – and hence cannot control – what is distributed by users, whether it be pornography or videos depicting gratuitous violence.

Over and above the examples we have already cited, there have many especially egregious examples of how this social media platform has been misused and abused. Two assailants of Jawaharlal Nehru University student Umar Khalid, one of them holding the Indian flag, proudly proclaimed their "achievement" on WhatsApp. The same platform was abused by Shambhulal Regar from Rajsamand, Rajasthan, to upload a gruesome video of himself brutally murdering a Muslim labourer from West Bengal.

Even as Ankhi Das wrote in *The Indian Express*, that there is "no place for terrorism and terrorist content on Facebook," the ability of individuals and groups to misuse its companion social media platform to disseminate highly problematic content – including disinformation for political purposes – remains undiminished. There is good reason to apprehend that such activities have picked up during the general elections.

13

Questions for Facebook

We reproduce below verbatim and unedited our questionnaire and the response we received from Facebook.

Questionnaire for Ankhi Das and Shivanth Thukral:

On Facebook India's policy team and Indian political parties

1. What is the nature of the relationship between Facebook (FB) India and political parties in the country? Which political parties does FB India liaise with?

2. Who in FB India is responsible for establishing and maintaining these relationships? How are these relationships structured? What are the terms of the agreements of such relationships? How much of these are in writing? Is it correct that most of requests made by political parties to FB India are not in writing?

3. What is the nature of engagement between FB's global politics and government outreach team headed by Katie Harbath and FB India's policy team headed by Ankhi Das and Shivnath Thukral? How much of these communications are in writing?

4. What is the structure of, and hierarchy in, FB India and its policy team? How many people are employed directly by the FB India policy team? What are their roles? Who in FB India liaises with political parties?

5. What is the volume and financial value of political advertisements placed on FB India and Instagram (IG) India? What percentage of the total advertising revenue of FB India and IG India does such revenue constitute?

6. How much of a revenue spike (in terms of percentage) are FB India and IG India expecting before the 2019 general elections?

7. Do particular pages on FB and handles on IG–like those of the Prime Minister of India, the PM's Office, government ministries and ministers–get preferential treatment in terms of reach and engagement? If the answer to the above question is "yes," which other pages get similar treatment in India?

8. Do representatives of political parties have access to dashboards, analytics and audience reports beyond page insights?

9. Under what heads and line items does FB India categorize sponsorships on its balance sheet?

10. Which team in FB India is responsible for sponsorships? Who heads this team?

Facebook India and the Bharatiya Janata Party

11. What is the nature of relationship between FB India and the Bharatiya Janata Party? What are the terms of engagement between FB India and the BJP? And how much of this is in writing? When was this relationship

established and who was responsible for establishing this relationship?

12. Who are the persons who liaise on behalf of FB India with the BJP and who are the persons who liaise on behalf of the BJP with FB India?

13. A senior BJP functionary who was responsible for the 2014 campaign and is currently associated the government has alleged that FB India and the BJP have a symbiotic relationship. How do you respond to his claim?

14. Has FB India organised consultancies, workshops, prepared reports for the BJP and its volunteers on how to use FB, IG and WhatsApp (WA) more effectively for political messaging on a large scale? When and on how many occasions in the recent past have such consultancies, workshops and reports been offered?

15. A former employee of FB India commenting on the relationship between FB India and the BJP claimed that FB India is run out of BJP's office at 11 Ashoka Road. How do you respond to such a claim?

Content moderation by Facebook India

16. Which year did FB India start moderating content? Who in FB India's policy team is responsible for content moderation?

17. Who in the policy team is responsible for community operations? Who does the risk and response team report to?

18. What are the categories of posts that are deemed worthy of a take-down on FB India?

19. Has FB India defined hate speech in the Indian context?

20. What are the categories of posts which have their reach reduced?

21. What are FB India, WA India and IG India's policies on hate speech, fake news and organised disinformation campaigns?

22. How do they differ from similar policies that Facebook has in other countries?

23. What are FB India's policies on content moderation? How strongly do FB or its contractors and associates enforce these policies in India as compared to other countries?

24. How does FB India moderate content? Which Indian think-tanks and non-government organisations did FB India consult or seek help from for making its content moderation guidelines.

25. What percentage of content moderation work happens in India? And how much content moderation work is outsourced?

26. Who are the third-party contractors who moderate content for FB in India?

27. How many local language content moderators does FB employ and in which languages?

28. What is the process followed for content moderation?

29. What categories of content are escalated to the International Compliance Unit of FB? How often does this take place?

30. What is the action taken on flagged content? What happens once a piece of content is flagged? What

happens once a piece of content is sought to be escalated after being flagged?

31. How often is content flagged? How often is action taken on flagged content?

32. Are there rules for what is allowed and what is not allowed on FB India? If so, is there a document outlining these rules that you would be willing to share with us?

33. What are the exceptions to the rule when it comes to content moderation?

34. Does FB India unilaterally take-down disinformation and fake news? Could you provide figures of instances of such take-down over the last five years?

35. What action has FB India taken so far to counter disinformation, fake news and hate speech?

36. How many content moderators does Facebook India directly employ? And how many content moderators does Facebook India outsource work to?

37. How many local language content moderators does Facebook India directly employ and how many is work outsourced to?

38. In the past six years, how many pages and posts were taken down at the behest of political parties, the Union government, the state governments and law enforcement agencies?

39. There have adverse comments on the time taken by FB to remove flagged content. *The New York Times*, *Reuters* and independent analysts have alleged that FB has taken weeks and months to remove flagged content in Myanmar and Sri Lanka. It has been further claimed

that content is only taken down by FB after the Western media reports on such content. What are your responses to these claims? What is the average turnaround time for taking down flagged India-specific content?

40. What are FB India's advertising policies for political advertisements and issue-based advertisements?

41. In the United States, FB has complied with provisions of the bill to amend the Honest Ads Act related to transparency in political advertisements. Does FB India intend to follow similar standards for political advertising in India?

42. The Election Commission of India is reportedly planning to bring political advertising on the social media under the category "paid news." Your views in this regard.

Right-wing groups "gaming" Facebook platforms

43. Ahead of the 2014 general elections, the BJP is said to have "gamed" your platforms – FB, IG and WA – to its advantage. It is claimed that the party and its affiliates continue to do so. How are you going to ensure that the BJP – or for that matter, any other political party – does not "misuse" or "abuse" your platforms ahead of the forthcoming general elections in India?

44. Does FB India know of and has observed the organised effort of right-wing groups to sow and spread disinformation and hate speech campaigns in India? If yes, what are the steps that have been taken, and will be taken, to counter organised disinformation campaigns?

45. The experience of the 2016 American elections has indicated to many that FB and IG can be "gamed" by

political parties to manipulate and change voting patterns and trends. How are FB, IG and WA planning to counter attempts at manipulating voter behaviour in India before the coming general elections scheduled for 2019?

46. Your security partners, Digital Forensics Research Lab and Fire Eye, and the global press have highlighted at least five instances (in South Africa, US, Brazil, Mexico and Cambodia) of coordinated disinformation campaigns originating in India. Has FB India observed other coordinated disinformation campaigns emanating from India?

47. Representatives of fact-checking organisations in India have alleged that FB India is not particularly keen on countering the spread of disinformation. What are your comments on such claims?

48. India does not have a significant fact-checking infrastructure. What can FB India do to strengthen this country's fact-checking infrastructure?

49. From 2013 till now, many incendiary and communally sensitive posts from India have got amplified on FB. Whereas FB India is proactive in taking down posts satirising the government and those that are critical of the government, how does FB India respond to the allegation that it has an asymmetric approach to content moderation?

50. *The Caravan* has claimed that FB India was less than proactive in allowing it to promote one of its articles on the business activities of Jai Amit Shah, the son of Amit Shah, president of the BJP. It has been claimed that the response FB India gave to *The Caravan* lacked credibility. What are your responses to such claims?

51. How many disinformation pages and handles, fake accounts and posts has FB India taken down to date? Are these details public? Are they available to journalists, external researchers for analysis? Please share whatever information you have in this regard.

52. Is it correct that the information on posts taken down by FB India does not correspond to the data put out by the government of India's Ministry of Electronics and Information Technology (MEITY)? If so, why are there discrepancies and mismatches?

53. Has FB India worked with the advertising agency Creativeland Asia?

54. There is a view that if Cambridge Analytica could have allegedly misused data gathered from Facebook, Facebook itself can do all that Cambridge Analytica did and much more with the data it has gathered from its users. What are your comments on such contentions?

Background Information on Personnel

55. What is Ankhi Das' role in Facebook India? What is her role in liaising with political parties, in particular, with the BJP?

56. When did FB India first get in touch with those responsible for Narendra Modi's campaign in 2013 before the 2014 general elections?

57. What has been Ankhi Das', Shivnath Thukral's and Katie Harbath's role in cultivating the relationship with the BJP and Narendra Modi?

58. How many times in the past six years have Ankhi Das,

Shivnath Thukral, Katie Harbath met Dr Hiren Joshi individually and together?

59. What were the agendas of each of these meetings?

60. We have reason to believe that Shivnath Thukral has known Dr Hiren Joshi, Anuj Gupta and Amit Malviya from 2013 onwards. We understand that he continues to maintain a close relationship with them. Is this correct?

61. A former campaign manager of the BJP has alleged that Shivnath Thukral was appointed to FB India at the behest of the Prime Minister's Office. How do you respond to this claim?

62. Was Shivnath Thukral's association with the Essar group controlled by the Ruia family, the "Mera Bharosa" initiative that was part of the Narendra Modi's pre-election campaign and his role as Managing Director, Carnegie India, taken into account when he was appointed FB's Policy Director for India?

63. What is FB India's relationship with *SheThePeople* with which Shaili Chopra is associated? Does FB India see no conflict of interest in financially supporting *SheThePeople*?

64. Who else other than Shivnath were interviewed, shortlisted for FB India policy director's position?

14

Facebook Responds

This was the response we received from a spokesperson of Facebook in India, which we reproduce below verbatim and unedited.

Statement on the working nature of the Policy team:

Facebook's policy team is focused on helping a variety of people – educators, our community, NGOs and governments – understand our policies, programs and products to help create positive and meaningful experiences for the people who use our services. We are globally invested in critical areas of internet governance and policy development – safety, small business growth, internet access, and giving people a voice. This team works with all political parties, and we work with all of them who reach out to us for trainings.

Facebook India and the Bhartiya Janata Party:

Our mission is to give people a voice in the issues that matter to them so they can build the communities they want. We do this by building tools that help people be informed voters in the lead up to elections, and by helping them find, follow, and connect with the people that represent them in government. An important part of our mission is equipping elected officials, candidates, and government organisations with the tools needed to connect and engage with their communities. Our Facebook politics and government team provides guidance and best practice to elected officials, governments, candidates and political parties around the globe on managing their own Facebook pages so that they can effectively engage with people in their countries. As part of the process they conduct training workshops for government officials and different departments as well as political parties both at national and state level.

Content moderation in India:

Our content policy team (not our India policy team) is responsible for developing our Community Standards (we have people in 11 offices around the world, including subject matter experts on issues such as hate speech, child safety and terrorism). We have a global Community Operations and Security team (including India) of 15,000 people (a mix of full-time employees, contractors and companies we partner with) around the world. As our 15,000-strong team grows to 20,000 by the end of the year, the number of content reviewers will grow with it.

Here are some useful links on our community standards:

https://newsroom.fb.com/news/2018/04/comprehensive-community-standards/

https://newsroom.fb.com/news/2018/07/hard-questions-content-reviewers/

On Hate Speech:

Our Community Standards are global, and we apply them consistently to our global community of 2.2 billion people. However, we are always looking for ways to evolve and improve these policies, and ensure they are responding to the type of abuse we are see on the platform.

Our hate speech policy, for example, defines hate speech as an attack on a person or group based on what we call their 'protected characteristics'. We define 'protected characteristics' as nationality, race, religion, ethnicity, gender, gender identity, sexual orientation, serious disability or disease. We recently evolved our hate speech policy in response to the kind of abuse we were seeing on the platform in India, and we added caste to our list of protected characteristics. This means that an attack on someone based on their caste would now violate our hate speech policy, and we would remove it when we become aware of it. We regularly talk to governments, community members, academics and other experts from around the globe to ensure that we are in the best position possible to recognize and remove such speech from our community.

Useful link:

https://www.facebook.com/communitystandards/hate_speech

Misinformation:

Misinformation is bad for people and bad for Facebook. We're making significant investments to stop it from spreading and to promote high-quality journalism and news literacy. Our strategy to stop misinformation on Facebook has three parts:

Remove accounts and content that violate our Community Standards or ad policies

Reduce the distribution of false news and inauthentic content

Inform people by giving them more context on the posts they see

Useful links:

https://newsroom.fb.com/news/2018/05/hard-questions-false-news/
https://newsroom.fb.com/news/2018/06/increasing-our-efforts-to-fight-false-news/

When Content is flagged:

When people report content, our Community Operations team reviews those reports based on our Community Standards[6], globally, in every time zone, and in more than 50 languages. We work with a global network of partners in locations around the world to ensure we have the right language expertise and can hire quickly in different time zones as new needs arise. We care deeply about the safety and security of the people who use Facebook – and for the people who do this work. Details of the content removed can be found on our transparency reports[7]

Removing content in Myanmar and Sri Lanka:

We've been too slow in places like Myanmar and Sri Lanka

---

6   https://www.facebook.com/communitystandards/
7   https://transparency.facebook.com/community-standards-enforcement

to deal with the hate and violence; as Mark (Zuckerberg) has said we need to take a broader view of our responsibilities, in particular in preventing abuse of our services. We are investing in people, technology, policies, programs to help address these very serious challenges in both Myanmar and Sri Lanka. Details on what we have done can be found on Myanmar:

https://newsroom.fb.com/news/2018/08/update-on-myanmar/

and

https://newsroom.fb.com/news/2018/08/removing-myanmar-officials/

Statement on Facebook and political ads:

As a strong supporter of transparency in political advertising, we are open about our political ads policies. We treat all parties advertising on Facebook equally. We take the time to review ads before allowing them on the platform. In order to do so, we require at least 24 hours to ensure the accuracy and validity of political ads.

For more details, our policy is outlined here:

https://www.facebook.com/policies/ads/restricted_content/political

Election Commission of India and "paid news":

We're taking significant steps to bring more transparency to ads and pages on Facebook. Anyone can now[8] view active

---

8   https://newsroom.fb.com/news/2018/06/transparency-for-ads-and-pages/

ads from pages on Facebook. The feature will allow our community in India and around the world - to see ads across Facebook, Instagram, Messenger and our partner network, even if those ads aren't shown to you. People can also learn more about pages, even if they don't advertise. For example, you can see any recent name changes and the date the page was created.

Removal of content in the past years includes what is reported to government:

We publish a report every 6 months on content removed, you can see details on content removed in the attached link below.

In our transparency report we only report content that has been geo-blocked in response to government take-down requests (restricted in the region).

When something on Facebook or Instagram is reported to us as violating local law, but doesn't go against our Community Standards, we may restrict the content's availability in the country where it is alleged to be illegal. We receive reports from governments and courts, as well from non-government entities such as members of the Facebook community and NGOs. This report details instances where we limited access to content based on local law.

https://transparency.facebook.com/community-standards-enforcement

Personnel information:

Ankhi (Das) is Facebook's Public Policy Director for India, Central and South East Asia. She and her team are focused on helping a variety of people – educators, our community, NGOs and governments – understand our policies, programs and products to help create positive and meaningful experiences for the people who use our services. As part of her role she and her team interact with several factions of the government.

We are globally invested in critical areas of internet governance and policy development – safety, small business growth, internet access, and giving people a voice. We have programs and initiative which we run globally (SheMeansBusiness, BoostYourBusiness, Think Before Your Share, our safety and mental health and suicide prevention programs).

On Hiring:

We are committed to building a workforce as diverse as the people and communities we serve, and our recruitment process reflects this. We focus on building a diverse slate of candidates for each role, and our recruitment process includes speaking with a variety of teams and stakeholders across the company to help determine a candidate's strengths and make sure we pick the right person for the job. Our goal is to hire the best people for the roles available, not just in India, but also globally. And this was the process followed for Shivnath's hiring.

On our relationship with SheThePeople:

SheThePeople has been associated with Facebook before Shivnath joined us.

Our program partnerships are subject to a compliance review that considers conflicts of interest and at the time of hiring all these reviews are mandatory.

15

Good Corporate Citizen?

After *NewsClick* published the five articles we wrote in November 2018, these were, our sources told us, discussed in the Prime Minister's Office and in Facebook India. The crisis in the organisation deepened and its public relations machinery got more active. It started partnering media organisations to spread awareness about how the social media could be misused and prominent advertisements were placed in leading dailies.

The government of India, on its part, has been pushing for an overhaul of intermediary liability rules (that govern the taking down of content on websites and blocking access to particular websites by internet service providers) and "safe harbour" provisions therewith. A safe harbour is a provision of a statute or a regulation that specifies that certain conduct will be deemed as not violating a particular rule. Thus, an internet service provider will argue that it should not be held liable if someone misuses its service by putting out objectionable content or acts in a manner deemed illegal.

With internet-based communication companies playing hardball, the Election Commission of India called for a meeting of representatives of such companies on 19 March 2019. After consultations, the Commission issued a set of guidelines for social networks and updated an application for citizens to report violations of the Model Code of Conduct (MCC). The code came into force a fortnight earlier, on 5 March, after the schedule for conducting elections was announced.

The day after the Election Commission met with represetatives of social media companies, on 20 March, the Internet and Mobile Association of India (IAMAI) put out a "voluntary code of ethics" ostensibly to ensure "free, fair and ethical usage of their platforms to maintain (the) integrity of (the) electoral process." The code urged "participants" to "endeavour to, where appropriate and keeping in mind the principle of freedom of expression… build awareness" about electoral laws and related instructions, develop a mechanism to notify the Election Commission of violations "within three hours" of being informed about the and thereafter take expeditious action.

Political advertisers would have to submit "pre-certificates" issued by the Election Commission or Media Certification and Monitoring Committees (MCMC) appointed by the Commission. In addition, social media platforms would have to conform to the rules laid down for other media (print and television), which specify that no political advertisements can be issued during the 48 hours period of "silence" or "curfew" preceding polling in a particular place.

The social media platforms, in effect, held the Election Commission responsible for certifying what are political advertisements online. The onus of pre-certification was on advertisers and not on intermediaries such as internet service providers and social media platforms like Facebook and WhatsApp, it was pointed out.

What this voluntary code overlooked were a few simple facts. The internet does not recognise geographical boundaries including national legal jurisdictions. Applying these rules become practically impossible especially when elections take place in multiple phases in different parts of the country. The other important issue that was raised related to the speed with which "offending" content should be taken down.

Electoral officers and retired civil servants, speaking at a public conference in New Delhi on 28 March that was moderated by one of the writers of this book (Paranjoy), were sceptical about the efficacy of the code of ethics and expressed unhappiness about why the entire exercise in regulating the social media had not commenced much earlier and not on the eve of the elections. As mentioned, the notification on the voluntary code came a fortnight after the MCC came into force.

K Mahesh, who is the District Electoral Officer of the East Delhi Lok Sabha constituency, raised various concerns about the voluntary code of ethics for the social media put out by the IAMAI. Why should the code be applicable only during the 48-hour period of silence before polling and not earlier, he asked, adding that the proposed channel of notification and communication would lead to "unnecessary and unwarranted" delay. He suggested that direct channels of communication be set up between the Election Commission and the returning officers (who are directly in charge of conducting the elections) and the heads of the MCMCs.

At the conference, former Information Technology

Secretary to the government of India Kamal K Jaswal described the code as an "act of tokenism" that was like a sieve filled with loopholes, a case of "too little too late." Even if political parties should not be expected to be proactive in suggesting ways in which the spread of fake news and propaganda on the social media could be checked, Jaswal felt the Election Commision acted "very coy" in using the plenary powers given to it under Article 324 of the country's Constitution – plenary powers are absolute powers granted to a body or an individual with no scope for the review of, or placing limtations on, the exercise of such powers. He added that was no adverse consequence for those who did not adhere to the voluntary code.

On the same occasion, former Chief Election Commissioner S Y Quraishi said the three-hour period for initiating action that had been suggested was just too long. "Three hours on the social media is an eternity," he quipped, agreeing with others who said that the corrective action contemplated could never be compared with the speed at which speed disinformation spreads. Quraishi asked: "How will you catch them (those who misuse and abuse the facilities offered by social media platforms)?"

The speakers at the conference also expressed their concerns that social media platforms would not be able to curb political advertising by "proxies" and by "pseudonymous" subscribers. Mahesh, an officer of the elite Indian Administrative Service, said there was a "big void" in the law and the rules governing the conduct of elections because there were no provisions for punitive action against those who disseminated content through proxy accounts and through volunteers. How this is done was elaborated in a *HuffPost India* investigation that is detailed in a later chapter.

Prabir Purkayastha, editor, *NewsClick* and a representative of the Free Software Movement of India said that since "virality" was what the social media platforms were striving for, expecting them to regulate themselves voluntarily was like asking a wolf to guard a herd of sheep.

Lawyer Apar Gupta of the Internet Freedom Foundation pointed out most social media companies had been tardy in appointing grievance officers who would act promptly on complaints from government authorities or on court orders. On the voluntary code of ethics, he was of the view that the Election Commission of India should have had wide-ranging consultations with various sections, including representatives of civil society organisations and digital activists, besides an industry association like the IAMAI whose members are arguably part of the problem being sought to be addressed.

Within days of the MCC coming into force, Facebook had a run-in with the election authorities. A show-cause notice was issued to a BJP leader Om Prakash Sharma (who is an elected member of the legislative assembly of Delhi from the Vishwas Nagar constituency) for putting up an advertisement on Facebook politicising the Pulwama attack by using his own photograph and those of other political leaders (including Prime Minister Modi and BJP president Amit Shah) together with a picture of Wing Commander Abhinandan Varthaman, the Indian Air Force (IAF) officer who had come back to India after his aircraft had crashed in Pakistan.

The Election Commission asked Shivnath Thukral, Facebook's Director, Public Policy for India and South Asia, to remove the advertisements shared by the BJP leader. His reported response was stunning. He asked what specific legal provisions had been violated by the disputed advertisement. Did he imply that the MCC lacked legal backing and that Facebook was hence not obliged to pull down the controversial advertisement?

The fact is that the Election Commission had issued a circular in December 2013 urging all political parties to "exercise great caution" while referring to the country's armed forces that are meant to be apolitical. It is also true that the Election Commission's MCC is a set of guidelines and norms relating to the conduct of elections – with respect to speeches, advertisements, manifestos, processions, campaigns and so on – have evolved with the consensus of all political parties in India who have consented to abide by the principles embodied in the code in letter and spirit. The code is to ensure that parties in power do not misuse their position of advantage to gain an unfair edge. For instance, the code states that candidates standing for elections should not make hateful speeches that pit one community against another or make false promises to influence voters.

A group of retired civil servants and civil society activists wrote to the Election Commission of India suggesting a slew of measures to constrain the social media during the general elections and prevent digital platforms from being misused and manipulated for political purposes in ways that would be work against the elections being free and fair. The Commission did not respond and on 5 April 2019, the text of a statement titled "Safeguarding Democracy from Digital Platforms" was released to the media – read the full text of the statement annexed at the end of this book.

What is evident to all but the most gullible is that few –
perhaps none – of the lofty goals laid down in the Model
Code of Conduct are likely to be adhered to by certain users
of the social media in India.

Meanwhile, the ruling party has gone on overdrive with
WhatsApp as its primary weapon of choice. While much of
the conversation on disinformation has focussed on Twitter and
Facebook, the biggest weapon for the BJP in the upcoming
election is WhatsApp. As stated, the app's architecture makes
it difficult to observe and map both information and its flow.
In September 2018, the BJP had announced that it is creating
a network of over 9,00,000 WhatsApp groups for its election
campaign. These groups are in addition to the hundreds of
thousands of other groups that the party already deploys,
formally and informally. While other political parties have woken
up to the BJP's social media strategies, their resources (both
human and financial) are relatively limited in comparison.

In February 2019, the Parliamentary Committee on
Information Technology summoned representatives of Twitter,
WhatsApp and Facebook to testify before it after prominent
accounts linked to the BJP were suspended for trolling and
issuing death threats. The Committee's meeting was attended
by eight of the committee's 22 members. Speaking to the
Quint on the summons, a committee member said "there is
no meaning in these meetings" that are "nothing but a waste
of public expenditure."

The same month, Carl Wong, WhatsApp's head of
communication, told the media in New Delhi that the

platform was being misused by political parties. While he did not name any specific political party, he told the news agency, the *Press Trust of India*: "We have seen a number of parties attempt to use WhatsApp in a way that was not intended and our firm message to them is using it in that way will result in bans of our service."

He also claimed that the company was detecting and removing two million WhatsApp accounts each month to prevent bulk messaging. Wong said:

> We have had the effort for the last several months where we have engaged with political parties to explain our firm view that WhatsApp is not a broadcast platform and is not a place to send messages at scale. And to explain to them that we will be banning accounts that engage in automated robotic behaviour and we do this regardless of the purpose of your account.

A number of academicians have termed the upcoming elections in India as one driven by WhatsApp. Phillipa Williams and Lipika Kamra, in an article titled "India's WhatsApp Election: Political parties risk undermining democracy with technology" published in *The Conversation*, claimed: "While parties across India's political spectrum – as well as globally – increasingly seek to gain from fake news by manipulating public opinion, the Hindu right has been far more successful at mobilising a common socio-political identity through media like WhatsApp," adding that the "steps taken by the company are a starting point but may not be enough."

While until early-2018, there were only four fact-checking initiatives in India, Facebook India now claims to have the biggest network of fact-checkers globally with seven partners and has made public an advertising archive to track pages and money spent on political advertising ahead of the election. The company is also spending on advertising campaigns across newspapers and the internet.

On 2 April 2019, WhatsApp announced the launch of its "Checkpoint Tipline" which appeared to be more an exercise in public relations than a tool to detect and delete disinformation, rumours, hate speech and incendiary content. WhatsApp had initially described it as a multi-lingual fact-checking service and later clarified the facility as "only... a means to collect information that is otherwise inaccessible given the nature of private messaging." It added:

> The Checkpoint tipline is primarily used to gather data for research, and is not a helpline that will be able to provide a response to every user. The information provided by users helps us understand potential misinformation in a particular message, and when possible, we will send back a message to users. We would like to verify every rumour but we know that will not be possible given the diversity of information we will receive and the limitations of any verification research.

WhatsApp clarified that any verification that is provided "will not be instant," and may take up to 24 hours to receive. A day after the announcement, *Buzzfeed* reported that the tipline was not a fact-checking service unlike what was being advertised.

16

Manipulating Algorithms?

On 30 January 2019, *The Caravan* published a detailed article by US-based digital activist and technologist Inji Pennu, in which it was argued that Facebook's community guidelines selectively policed content that was against Narendra Modi and his government. Dozens of examples were cited about how individual accounts and Facebook pages were shut out of the social media platform ostensibly for violating the organisation's Community Standards but which fell into a distinct pattern – those in favour of the Modi regime were spared whereas those opposed to it were inconvenienced, often without explanation.

The writer caustically remarked: "Facebook thrives as a banana republic of the digital world. Digital-rights groups have been requesting to audit Facebook's Community Standards and algorithms for years due to its caustic social impact, to no avail."

Instances are given on how Facebook's decisions to take-down content revealed a sexist and misogynistic pattern:

After my story about the threats women were facing on Facebook for speaking up was published, the perpetrators instantly turned towards me. They issued threats targeting my family and even threatened to choke me at Miami Beach, where I was then living. One posted a picture with a noose around my neck. I contacted Facebook Forums – a space created by Facebook for users – and asked them to take-down the threatening posts. However, instead of helping me, Facebook suspended my profile. It was highly likely that my profile had been reported, as the threats I received had talked about taking it down.

When my profile was taken down, I tried to log back in, but was unsuccessful. To date, Facebook does not have a system of prior warnings that lets users know that their profile may be suspended for a particular reason. The person whose profile has been suspended is immediately logged out; they are then requested to contact the Facebook Community Center. When I contacted the community centre, Facebook asked me to submit my government identification. I refused.

Pennu claims that "the person of contact from Facebook for Indian profiles, Shruti Moghe, Facebook's Policy Programs Manager for India and South Asia, would sometimes disappear and refuse to respond until I added Facebook's policy heads, such as Antigone Davis, the head of global safety, and (Monika) Bickert, (head of product policy and counterterrorism at Facebook) to the mail trails."

The writer provides examples of rape threats against left-wing activist Kavita Krishnan in May 2016: "...I reached out to Bickert...(who) wrote me a lengthy email, stating that Facebook was a safe place for women, but that it had a different set of community guidelines for 'celebrity' women…(and) refused to take-down the post threatening Krishnan."

In the instance of Rajiv Tyagi, a former officer of the Indian Air Force, his Facebook account was suspended twice, in 2016 and in 2018.

> His posts are popular for their scathing criticism of the Modi government. On 24 August 2018, he was blocked for 30 days for calling out a profile of a user who appeared to be right-leaning. In his email to me (Pennu), he wrote, "I have been blocked for commenting in a discussion thread on my wall, words to the effect, 'Why do you have an orange *bandar* (monkey in Hindi) as your DP (or display picture)? I thought we had evolved from monkeys a long time ago...'! ... I cannot imagine how such a comment violates Facebook's 'Community Standards' so violently, that I get blocked for 30 days!"

Other examples cited are those of *Vartha Bharati*, a Kannada daily, and *BFirst*, a liberal news portal. Pennu writes that these portals and publications "even lost the money they spent on Facebook advertisements because their profiles were suspended and they could not get any traffic." In April 2018, before the assembly elections in Karnataka, Feku Express, a Facebook page with more than 512,000 followers, many of whom were from Karnataka, was also taken down. It was alleged that the portal had published pornographic content but this was denied and, according to the writer, never established. Other instances provided by Pennu pointed towards an alarming state of affairs.

On 2 July 2018, I was alerted to a Facebook Live broadcast, where five Hindu right-wing men were asking Hindus to rampantly kill Muslims. Since the live video was broadcasted on the Uttar Pradesh chief minister Adityanath's page, it was shared widely. The link was taken down after a few hours by Facebook, after several users complained about it. But nothing happened to the page; it remained intact, and one of the users, Surendra Singh, who shared the live video asking people to kill Muslims, is still on the platform. How is it that none of Facebook's checkpoints of violence, hate speech or safety are applicable in the case of Hindutva pages?

Similarly, there is the case of Deepak Sharma, a Facebook user from Rajasthan, who constantly posts hate speech against Muslims and women. He uses Facebook Live often and constantly threatens to wipe out Muslims. On 16 December 2018, he posted a video with similar threats. The video now has 77,000 views, 1,056 shares, 980 comments and 1,400 reactions. I, along with a few other digital activists, reported this post using Facebook's community guidelines. Facebook responded that the content of the video does not go against their community guidelines – the standard response to Hindutva hate pages. How is it that Facebook cannot monitor such hate content when anything against Narendra Modi or the alternative right is taken down immediately?

The writer argues that Facebook's algorithms are written and manipulated in a manner to drown critical voices, concluding:

Evidently, activists critical of the government are losing their voice on social media against Facebook's black-box policies.

Speaking with activists, I have observed that once a profile is out of the feeds for 30 days, its earlier fiery vigour is also lost. This is the carrot and stick, where freedom of speech is curtailed randomly and frequently without fully stopping it and the information dissemination velocity is lost.

In 2015, while meeting with Bickert and her team, I discussed the gaps in Facebook's policing of right-wing fundamentalists groups, women activists facing death and rape threats. I was trying to impress upon them that Facebook's approach was woefully inadequate to understand the cultural sensitivity of India, the colloquial and native language nuances, and how the FAQs (frequently asked questions) on community guidelines would not work. Ankhi Das, who is Facebook's Public Policy Director for South Asia, snapped back at me, "You are living in US, you won't understand India." Maya Leela, an activist who is also a friend, was present there and heard Das's response. Das's retort sounded familiar to me – it was the language of Hindutva trolls.

On 28 March 2019, the Department of Housing and Urban Development of the US government filed charges against Facebook for discriminatory advertising that violated the Fair Housing Act. It has been alleged that Facebook's advertisements discriminated against users on the basis of their race, religion, gender and ethnicity in the first lawsuit of its kind in the US.

In April 2019, *The NewsMinute*, reported that Facebook's advertising systems allowed caste-based targeting in India. "Unlike real-world discrimination which is visible, and can be exposed, and fought against, a lot of the discrimination on platforms such as Facebook happens in the background," the report quoted the researcher who spotted the ad-targetting parameters. The report further quoted, Alok Prasanna Kumar, a senior resident fellow at Vidhi Centre for Legal Policy who explained that Indian laws understand discrimination only through the context of untouchability nor do the laws take into account discrimination in private spaces. "Thus, the discriminatory practices of Facebook would go unchecked in India," the report added.

17

Aftermath of Pulwama

India's infrastructure to counter false information in the run-up to the elections was tested in the immediate aftermath of the deaths of 40 Central Reserve Police Force (CRPF) personnel in a suicide bombing attack in Pulwama in Jammu & Kashmir on 14 February 2019 masterminded by a Pakistan-based terror outfit that claimed responsibility for the killings. The Indian Air Force retaliated by entering Pakistani airspace in the Balakote area near the Line of Control. An Indian fighter plane was shot down and the pilot, Wing Commander Abhinandan Varthaman was held captive for 60 hours before he was allowed to return to India.

While India and Pakistan appeared for a while to be at the brink of a war, the BJP's propaganda machinery was at work in full swing. Within hours of the terror attack in Pulwama, messages starting circulating on WhatsApp and Facebook in huge numbers targeting the ruling party's and Modi's political opponents, particularly Rahul Gandhi and Priyanka Gandhi of the Indian National Congress. Video footage from Syria and Iraq were circulated claiming that these were videos of the terror attack and old videos of military drills were widely distributed. Trushar Barot, head of Facebook's "election integrity team" who used to earlier work with the BBC, was taken aback by the sheer scale of the operation. He exclaimed on Twitter: "I've never seen anything like this before – the scale of fake content circulating on one story."

An investigation by Kunal Purohit titled "After Pulwama terror attack, WhatsApp groups are fuelling hypernationalism, hatred and warmongering" published by *Firstpost* claimed that most of such messages had originated in WhatsApp groups linked to the BJP:

> One crucial message constantly made the rounds: a "request" to Prime Minister Narendra Modi to go to war with Pakistan as fitting retribution for the Pulwama attack. This message was spotted in various groups. The "request" ends with an assurance to Modi that the country would reward him for the war by giving him 400 seats in the upcoming Parliamentary elections.

Eleven days after the Pulwama incident, India retaliated. Within minutes of the news of the IAF entering Pakistani airspace becoming public, memes, infographics with misinformation, patriotic messages and multimedia extolling Modi and the BJP flooded WhatsApp, Facebook and other internet-based communication networks. For nearly half a month, much of such dubious information circulating on the internet found their way to mainstream newspapers, television news channels and their websites. One such video – put out by *Asian News International (ANI), News18, India Today, ABP News, Times*

Now, Dainik Bhaskar, Dainik Jagran, India TV and *Zee News*, all of which are media organisations that are, by and large, sympathetic to the BJP – claimed that the Pakistan Army had admitted that 200 terrorists were killed by the IAF in the 26 February strike. The video depicting a Pakistani soldier or civilian being buried was intentionally shown out of context, according to an investigation by fact-checking website *AltNews*.

Ravi Shankar Prasad, India's Union Minister for Electronics and Information Technology, who has been at the forefront of issuing threats to internet-based communication networks for the proliferation of misinformation and disinformation, also used the dubious video to attack Rahul Gandhi while praising television channels for producing proof of India having attacked Pakistan. He said: "… there is so much evidence today in the public domain. On behalf of the party, I want to thank TV channels that they kept the full evidence in front of the country. We are very proud of all television channels."

The claim of casualties in Pakistan following India's retaliatory strike has been contested by international news agencies and outlets like *Reuters* and *The New York Times*. The government of India has not released any information officially on the number of deaths on account of India's retaliatory action. The volume of disinformation that followed the Pulwama–Balakote episodes indicated that the moves made by the social media platforms in controlling their dissemination were woefully insufficient and inadequate. In fact, an investigation by *AltNews* showed that Facebook's "fact-checking" partners were themselves circulating misinformation. The report titled "3 out of Facebook's 7 fact-checking partners have shared misinformation post-Pulwama" opined: "That the misreports were published by fact-checking outlets at a time when public emotions were most susceptible to getting misled is unfortunate."

Pratik Sinha of the Ahmedabad-based fact-checking, fake news-busting website *AltNews*, in an interview commented on how the propaganda on the social media had multiple objectives.

>...the first figure that was bandied about was this figure of 300 terrorists that have been killed by the IAF strike... Now as soon as that happened... multiple pictures of dead bodies started circulating on social media claiming that these are the people who have been killed by the IAF strike. We recently did a detailed story on 12 pictures where we showed how each one of these pictures are of either a previous bomb blast somewhere else or (an) earthquake... (these were) circulated claiming that this is the amount of destruction (by)... the Indian Air Force...

One of the first videos circulated after the IAF strike was that of a missile hitting a building and blowing it to smithereens, he stated. It was claimed that these visuals were genuine but were actually from a video game. Sinha said that social media platforms were whipping up jingoism and refusing to raise questions that were uncomfortable as far as the Indian government is concerned:

>... for example, in an interview of a mother of a slain CRPF soldier the very day when the IAF strike happened, she (says that) the dead bodies of our sons were taken around everywhere... (but) I don't see a single dead body

of a terrorist... When you claim a number of 300... a government can possibly hide four, five, six or ten bodies, but (in the)... the age of-front facing cameras, how do you hide 300 bodies...?

As an example of how disinformation was circulated widely by the mainstream media, Sinha pointed out that the most widely circulated daily newspaper in his state, the *Gujarat Samachar*, put out a story with a big bold headline that suggested that Modi had "blown off" 350 terrorists.

He said that it was easy to misuse social media to influence the gullible. After the Pulwama attack, a picture was put out depicting Rahul Gandhi with the suicide bomber. To Sinha's trained eyes, the picture was "clearly photo-shopped" but a cab driver his friend met showed him the same picture and remarked how Rahul Gandhi was with the man "who killed 40 of our soldiers." "So that is the penetration of misinformation," he said, adding that there is a substantial section of our population which does not have the ability to distinguish between what is genuine and what is fake.

On 6 April 2019, in an article titled "WhatsApp: The 'black hole' of fake news in India's election," Kevin Ponniah of BBC News wrote how his organisation's fact-checkers found that the pictures – purportedly of dead militants and a destroyed training camp – circulated after the Balakote attack were "old images that were being shared with false captions." He stated: "One photo showed a crowd of Muslim women and men gathered around three bodies but those pictured were actually victims of a suicide attack in Pakistan in 2014. A series of photos – of crumbling buildings, piles of debris and bodies in shrouds lying on the ground – were traced to a devastating earthquake in Pakistan-administered Kashmir in 2005."

★ ★ ★

There is little evidence so far to support claims by internet-based communication networks that their response to bad information has reduced the circulation of such information. If anything, the distribution of misinformation and disinformation after the Pulwama and Balakote attacks indicates that the BJP and its cadre of supporters and volunteers are responsible for misusing these technologies with impunity and that Facebook and WhatsApp have done little or nothing to contain the misuse despite loud claims to the contrary.

With the ruling party being the biggest producer and distributor of disinformation in India, the shadow-boxing by the government of India and the public relations efforts by internet-based communication networks is only expected to get louder. The unanswered question is to what extent the social media warriors of the current ruling dispensation in India will be successful in influencing political preferences. This will be known only after the results of the 17th Lok Sabha elections are announced on 23 May 2019.

18

On Overdrive

As elections approached, representatives of Facebook as well as its critics went on overdrive.

Contrary to the claims made by the digital monopolies Google and Facebook that their companies are essentially "tech" companies and not "news" organisations, the simple fact is that more and more people across the world and also in India were getting news from social media platforms. A study by the Reuters Institute for the Study of Journalism found that over half (52 per cent) of the English-language users of the internet in India who had been surveyed said they got news on Facebook and WhatsApp.

Not surprisingly, politicians and political parties have become brands to be micro-targeted by social media platforms that have become relatively more important in constituencies where the contest is expected to be keen and the margins of victory/defeat likely to be thin.

As on 21 March 2019, according to Facebook's Ad Library, more than 30,000 political advertisements had been published relating to India on which an estimated ₹6.54

crore had been spent. Total ad spend on social media in India has jumped: from $0.5 million in 2014 this figure is expected to rise to over $25 million in 2019. According to the IAMAI, all political parties would spend nearly 6 per cent of their total election budget on advertising on social media platforms.

Between 7 February and 2 March 2019, approximately 70 per cent of the total ad expenditure on Facebook that was made public went to the Indian government, the BJP and pro-BJP pages. Among the state governments led by parties other than the BJP, the highest ad spending was by the Karnataka government and the Chief Minister of Odisha Naveen Patnaik.

Facebook's weekly ad library report for the 17–23 March 2016 period indicates that "My First Vote for Modi" spent the most (₹46.6 lakh) on what were deemed to be political advertisements. Next came advertisements for the YSR Congress Party in Andhra Pradesh by Prashant Kishor's Indian Political Action Committee (₹17.52 lakh) followed by the BJP's "Bharat Ke Mann Ki Baat" (₹9.68 lakh) about which there is more later. In the previous week, the second position had been held by the pro-BJP Facebook page "Nation With NaMo" (₹17.7 lakh).

Voters were lured with freebies like badges, T-shirts, bags, mobile phone covers, caps if they "pledged" their first vote for Modi – the merchandise were available for sale on the official website of the Prime Minister as well. *AltNews* estimated that since February 2019, the two pages had spent ₹1.8 crore on political advertisements, and wondered if the expenditure would be disclosed in the accounts of the BJP that would be submitted to the Election Commission and whether such expenditure could be interpreted as "illegal" attempts to "unduly influence" voters.

★ ★ ★

On 3 April 2019, the instant messaging platform WhatsApp announced that its users would have the option of choosing whether or not they wanted to be part of a group by introducing a new privacy setting. Earlier, a user could be added to any group without her or his consent. In a statement, the Facebook-owned company said: "WhatsApp groups continue to connect family, friends, coworkers, classmates and more. As people turn to groups for important conversations, users have asked for more control over their experience."

No mention was made of how WhatsApp groups were being used to manipulate political opinion, or what Facebook describes as "coordinated inauthentic behaviour" (CIB) and uncoordinated "civic spam" involving single users with multiple accounts (SUMA) – displaying technology companies' love for acronyms. But the actions of the social media giant indicated that it was indeed feeling the pinch of criticism.

On 28 March, Facebook took down some 11,000 political advertisements published by Helo, a Chinese App. According to the news website, *The Print*, the advertisements taken down referred to politicians and political issues without carrying a disclaimer about who had paid for the advertisements – aggregating ₹7.7 crore. Among the bits of fake news circulated by Helo was one alleging that the BBC had called the Congress the "fourth most corrupt party in the world" and another alleging that Congress leader from Rajasthan Sachin

Pilot had said that India should have helped Pakistan clear its debts instead of investing in the Statue of Unity or the statue of Vallabhbhai Patel in Gujarat.

Facebook says it has made mandatory from February 2019 that all political advertisements should carry a disclaimer. According to its own data, the most "popular" page on the platform was one titled "My First Vote for Modi" followed by "Bharat Ke Mann Ki Baat" (literally translated to mean "what's inside the mind of Bharat" and closely resembling the title of Prime Minister Modi's radio programme "Mann Ki Baat" loosely translated to mean "what's in my mind") and "Nation With NaMo." On the second named page, a sum of ₹1.15 crore had been spent on 2,498 advertisements with disclaimers while ₹1.08 crore had been spent on 1,227 advertisements without disclaimers.

The activities of those accessing these Facebook pages, despite their overt political leanings, were nevertheless innocuous compared to others. The "We Support Narendra Modi" public group and the Facebook page "Yogi Sarkar" (meaning Yogi Government apparently referring to the government of India's most populous state Uttar Pradesh led by Chief Minister Yogi Adityanath) both shared a photoshopped picture of Congress leader Sonia Gandhi sitting on the lap of former President of the Maldives Abdul Gayoom.

Caught in the crossfire was Ashish Gupta, a government officer working with the Department of Telecommunications, who wrote to the Commissioner of Police, Delhi, complaining about an "inflammatory" video circulated on WhatsApp that was allegedly instigating people to attack Kashmiris. The video had been prepared by Kapil Mishra, a politician who had fallen out with the leadership of the Aam Aadmi Party. Gupta's action was criticised by right-wing websites like *OpIndia* and Facebook pages like "True Indology" and "Batmanbabu" – instead of acting on his complaint, he was suspended from his job for allegedly misusing his official letterhead to write to the Delhi Police chief, a classic case of shooting the messenger.

The popular anti-BJP producer of videos on YouTube, Dhruv Rathee, found that he had been briefly "banned" by Facebook for tangentially suggesting that there were similarities between Adolf Hitler and India's Prime Minister.

On All Fool's Day 2019, Facebook's head of cybersecurity policy Nathaniel Gleicher, put out a detailed statement on actions taken in Pakistan and India which is worth quoting at length:

> We have removed pages, groups and accounts for violating Facebook's policies on coordinated inauthentic behaviour or spam. Today's action includes four separate take-down – each distinct and unconnected.

> We removed 687 Facebook pages and accounts – the majority of which had already been detected and suspended by our automated systems – that engaged in coordinated inauthentic behaviour in India and were linked to individuals associated with an IT Cell of the Indian National Congress.

> • We removed 15 Facebook pages, groups and accounts that

engaged in coordinated inauthentic behaviour in India and were linked to individuals associated with an Indian IT firm, Silver Touch.

- We removed 321 Facebook pages and accounts in India that have broken our rules against spam. Unlike the first three actions, this last activity does not represent a single or coordinated operation – instead, these are multiple sets of pages and accounts that behaved similarly and violated our policies.

We have detailed each of these actions below.

Coordinated Inauthentic Behaviour Enforcement

The operations we found to be engaged in coordinated inauthentic behaviour were two distinct sets of activity in India and one network in Pakistan. We didn't find any links between the campaigns we've removed today, but they used similar tactics by creating networks of accounts to mislead others about who they were and what they were doing.

We are constantly working to detect and stop coordinated inauthentic behaviour because we don't want our services to be used to manipulate people. **We're taking down these pages and accounts based on their behaviour, not the content they posted**. In each case detailed below, the people behind this activity coordinated with one another and used fake accounts to misrepresent themselves, and that was the basis for our action.

While we are making progress rooting out this abuse, as we've said before, it's an ongoing challenge and we're committed to continuously improving to stay ahead. That means building better technology, hiring more people and working more closely with law enforcement, security experts and other companies.

In each case below, we identified violating accounts and pages through ongoing internal investigations into coordinated inauthentic behaviour in the region ahead of the upcoming elections in India. We have shared relevant information with policymakers and technology platforms.

India

The individuals behind this activity used fake accounts, the majority of which had already been detected and suspended by our automated systems, and joined various groups to disseminate their content and increase engagement on their own pages. The page admins and account owners typically posted about local news and political issues, including topics like the upcoming elections, candidate views, the INC and criticism of political opponents including the Bharatiya Janata Party (BJP). While the people behind this activity attempted to conceal their identities, our review found that it was connected to individuals associated with an INC IT Cell.

- *Presence on Facebook:* 138 pages and 549 Facebook accounts.

- *Followers:* About 206,000 accounts followed one or more of these pages.

- *Advertising:* Around $39,000 USD in spending for ads on Facebook, paid for in Indian rupees. The first ad ran in August 2014 and the most recent ad ran in March 2019.

Separately, we removed 15 pages, groups and accounts for engaging in coordinated inauthentic behaviour on Facebook and Instagram in India. A small number of page admins and account owners used a combination of authentic and fake accounts to share their content across a variety of pages. They posted about local news and political events, including topics like the Indian government, the upcoming elections, the BJP and alleged misconduct of political opponents including the INC. Although the people behind this activity attempted to conceal their identities, our investigation found that this activity was linked to individuals associated with an Indian IT firm, Silver Touch.

- *Presence on Facebook and Instagram:* 1 page, 12 Facebook accounts, 1 group and 1 Instagram account.

- *Followers:* About 2.6 million accounts followed this page, about 15,000 accounts joined this group, and around 30,000 accounts followed this Instagram account.

- *Advertising:* Around $70,000 USD in spending for ads on Facebook, paid for in Indian rupees. The first ad ran in June 2014 and the most recent ad ran in Feb 2019.

Removing Additional Pages and Accounts that Violate our Spam and Misrepresentation Policies in India

We also removed 227 pages and 94 accounts in India for violating our policies against spam and misrepresentation. These policies, outlined in Facebook's Community Standards, are designed to help make sure people can trust the connections they make on Facebook and are not misled about the content they are seeing. These pages and accounts were engaging in behaviours that expressly violate our policies. This included using fake accounts or multiple accounts with the same names; impersonating someone else; posting links to malware; and posting massive amounts of content across a network of groups and pages in order to drive traffic to websites they are affiliated with in order to make money. Unlike the take-downs for coordinated inauthentic behaviour, this activity was not part of one coordinated operation.

We routinely remove accounts and pages that engage in this type of harmful, often financially-motivated, behaviour – like ads for fraudulent products or fake weight loss "remedies." The people behind this behaviour create pages using fake accounts or multiple accounts with the same names. They post clickbait posts on these pages to drive people to websites that are entirely separate from Facebook and seem legitimate, but are actually ad farms. The people behind the activity also post the same clickbait posts in dozens of Facebook groups, often hundreds of times in a short period, to drum up traffic for their websites. And they often use their fake accounts to generate fake likes and shares. This artificially inflates engagement for their inauthentic pages and the posts they share, misleading people about their popularity and improving their ranking in News Feed.

This activity goes against what people expect on Facebook and it violates our policies. This is why we continue to invest in people and resources to improve the technology we use to detect this type of harmful behaviour, and we will continue to take action on an ongoing basis to address it.

The section of the media in India that is favourably inclined towards Modi, BJP and his government predictably highlighted the references to the Congress, omitting and/or downplaying the fact that Gleicher's statement merely mentioned Silver Touch, forgetting to mention the firm's close association with the Modi government – it has developed the NaMo application and the App for Rashtrapati Bhavan, the official residence of the President of India.

Commentators like Anita Gurumurthy and Jai Vipra, who work with the non-government organization, IT For Change, argued in *Firstpost* on 5 April, 2019:

> Appearing to cause trouble in elections does not augur well for Facebook's reputation, and so, it does have a business interest in maintaining/appearing to maintain fairness. And while Facebook's actions might be legitimate according to its own policies, we must not uncritically accept its self-appointed role as the custodian of Indian democracy. The platforms that Facebook controls – including WhatsApp – have now become an infrastructural service provided to countries around the world. And Facebook is technically not accountable to the people of these countries for how it manages this infrastructural service.

> Facebook is a company incorporated in the US, and as such is only accountable to the US government. The implication of the infrastructural nature of its service is that – as a platform that co-creates the public sphere encompassing not just ordinary people, but their political representatives and the lobbies that make and break political power, no individual or political party can afford to ignore it.

> Even if Facebook faces flak, as it did after the infamous Cambridge Analytica scandal, any reputational damage it may suffer in real terms is pretty much contained, thanks to its monopoly power. Facebook could, therefore act in allegedly

fair and noble ways or not; it could choose to censor that which is inauthentic or not.

Gurumurthy and Vipra pointed out that Facebook lacked accountability to the Indian electorate and also lacked transparency. They added perceptively that they did not know whether Facebook was telling the truth about why it took down these pages, who were the people who controlled these pages, and whether their behaviour was really "inauthentic and coordinated." Furthermore, it was also not known which other pages were allowed to stay on despite exhibiting coordinated inauthentic behaviour simply because "Facebook controls how much data it releases about these actions."

The writers were of the opinion that the "glaring lacunae in the accountability and transparency of the infrastructure scaffolding the public sphere become more worrisome because they directly impact Indian democracy." They added:

In the digital age, social media platforms are co-implicated in how society's democratic contours evolve. Decisions by platform companies deeming certain activity authentic and certain others inauthentic beg the question about who determines what action is good for democracy. Facebook's acts of selective commission and omission are part of its pick-and-mix game to use shifting standards as may be best for its business and in utter disregard of local laws. The fine line between content and behaviour may amount to nothing significant for social good and completely ignore democratic consensus about the same.

Gurumurthy and Vipra recalled how in the Kathua rape case, the Delhi High Court had issue notices to Facebook, Google, YouTube and Twitter, for disclosing the identity of the victim in contravention of India's law. They said Facebook's "external oversight board" had not been democratically constituted and had only advisory powers. Besides transparency on spending on advertisements, there was need for "mandatory" public disclosure of decisions on "allowing, promoting, and limiting content." They wrote:

> Platforms make trade-offs between free speech and safety/anti-racism/counter-democratic speech, and these trade-offs are often made algorithmically. Transparency will help citizens understand what choices were made and demand different choices, if they so desire.

The writers believe that if the Indian government changes its rules governing intermediary liability, Facebook would have no choice but to reveal its data. The point towards the law passed in France in December 2018 that *inter alia* requires digital platforms that exceed a certain number of hits in a day to disclose their algorithms. They concluded their article stating:

> The solution to its lack of accountability, of course, will have a much longer path. The Indian Parliament does not have the same ability to summon Facebook to a hearing as the US Congress does. Nevertheless, we must demand that democratic oversight over digital platforms like Facebook be maintained in the case of elections through the Election Commission

of India, or through a Parliamentary Standing Committee comprising members from ruling and opposition parties.

A week after Facebook released its report on taking down pages engaged in coordinated inauthentic behaviour in India, fact-checking website *AltNews* investigated the company's claims. In an article titled, "Facebook purge: The curious case of pages that did not feature in FB press release," Pooja Chaudhuri found glaring omissions in the press release issued by the social network:

> *AltNews* found that the take-down of pro-BJP pages wasn't limited to 'The India Eye'. We discovered hundreds of other pages which published content in favour of the ruling party and were recently removed by Facebook.

> A similar observation was made with regard to pro-Congress pages. Though their number was smaller, several Congress-supporting accounts, recently taken down by Facebook, found no mention in its statement.

The greatest hit of the Facebook purge were pages and accounts linked to the BJP. Speaking to the *Quartz India*, Ben Nimmo of the Digital Forensic Research Laboratory (DFRL) said, "The big difference was that the INC operation could afford to lose some of its pages without putting a big dent in its overall operation. The take-down of the pro–BJP pages will have much more impact on the overall operation, because their followings were so much bigger."

It is curious why FB played down the purge of pro-BJP pages. Chaudhuri adds in her *AltNews* article:

Facebook has partnerships with fact-checking websites in India for many months now. Why weren't pages/accounts who are serial offenders in the area of misinformation not taken down as well? The Facebook release clearly mentions that the take-down was not based on content. Facebook needs to bring in more transparency toward an action that might significantly influence elections in India. Furthermore, it is concerning that a platform which claims sincerity in its effort to deter misinformation has not identified routine purveyors of disinformation and made them a part of the recent take-down.

On 4 April 2019, *HuffPost India* published a detailed investigation that was provocatively titled: "How Modi and (Amit) Shah Turned A Women's NGO Into A Secret Election Propaganda Machine." The article written by Samarth Bansal, Gopal Sathe, Rachna Khaira and Aman Sethi, pointed out how a relatively obscure organisation called the Association of Billion Minds (ABM) was working as the BJP president's "personal election unit," recommending candidates who are standing for elections, running the "Nation with NaMo" application and creating fake news.

In an earlier avatar named the Sarvani Foundation, ABM had been set up on the advice of political strategist Prashant Kishor before the 2014 Lok Sabha elections ostensibly as an NGO to empower women, notably survivors of acid attacks. After lying dormant for three years, the organisation "tasked Dipak Patel, a discreet Gujarati businessman, and Himanshu Singh, a 31-year-old former McKinsey consultant, with assembling a cohort of IIT (Indian Institute of Technology)

141

engineers, consultants, lawyers and young professionals, to become BJP party president Shah's personal election consulting unit."

The *HuffPost India* article claims ABM has been working as a "secretive quorum of nerds... running sophisticated misinformation campaigns to spread fake news and false claims on social media and WhatsApp and in staged conversations in public gatherings. ABM's campaigns – which are often communal and divisive – are ramped up on the eve of critical elections and throttled down in the interludes between polls, even as the BJP has maintained a public distance from the firm."

In March 2018, Amit Malviya, the head of BJP's IT Cell, claimed he didn't know about ABM on a public occasion. The organisation reportedly has a "team of at least 161 full-time employees in 12 regional offices across India (that) provides the BJP with feedback on its key political moves, helps shortlist candidates for vital elections, and manages a phalanx of paid field workers who introduce themselves to party cadre as 'Amit Shah's team'."

This group conceives, designs, executes and prepares memes for many of the BJP's campaigns, including "Main Bhi Chowkidar," "Nation with NaMo", and "Bharat Ke Mann Ki Baat." These are menes made to go viral across a network of Facebook pages with millions of followers.

Two ABM-managed pages are the top two biggest spenders on Facebook, a fact disclosed once the social network rolled out its advertiser transparency campaign in February 2019. Yet, ABM's covert online presence shows how Facebook's transparency campaign is easily subverted.

HuffPost India analysed hundreds of pages of company records, election expenditure statements and website registries, and interviewed 20 people, including former and serving ABM employees, former associates of the company's founders, and on-ground staff, to illustrate how India's cash-rich ruling party has married Silicon Valley tech platforms with a deep pool of paid workers and unpaid party cadres to assemble a formidable election machine. The machine has many moving parts but a single purpose: to bombard India's 900 million voters with a relentless stream of real and fake information to ensure all attention is always focused on one man – Narendra Modi.

To this end, ABM plays a role in every aspect of the BJP's election planning. The firm compiles detailed dossiers on potential candidates from each constituency, prepares poll booth-level political intelligence reports, plots out routes for teams canvassing for votes, runs polling day war-rooms, and designs and manages online propaganda campaigns.

HuffPost India quoted Jagdeep Chhokar, co-founder of the Association of Democratic Reforms, saying: "I would characterise the use of consultancies by any political party as an act of subterfuge, but it cannot be termed illegal... It is immoral but not illegal."

Sahana Udupa, who teaches digital politics at the University of Munich, was also quoted saying: "The collusion between data surveillance capital and political power is deeply damaging for democracy, since voters' behavioural patterns are traced, plotted, predicted and played upon in surreptitious and covert ways."

The portal said it had used cyberforensic tools to establish links between ABM and pages identified by the fact-checking website, *BOOMLive* – like *Express Bangalore*, *Bangalore Herald*, *Bengaluru Mirror* and *Bengaluru Times* – that had "peddled political propaganda" and posted "inflammatory content" against the political opponents of the BJP before the Karnataka elections in 2018. These websites had published "fake survey results that were attributed to fictitious polling agencies, predicting a massive victory for the BJP" and after the party failed to form the government in the state, the sites disappeared.

The *Bangalore Herald* page on Facebook, *BOOMLive* found, was redirecting to *Bharatpositive.in*, a website and Facebook page with close to one million followers that consistently published pro-BJP content and fake news. In November 2018, it put out on Facebook a post falsely claiming that money donated to the family of an eight-year-old Muslim girl, who was brutally gang-raped and murdered in J&K's Kathua, had been stolen by Shehla Rashid, a vocal opponent of Prime Minister Modi.

Bharatpositive was set up in August 2017 by Nikhil Mehra, who was an ABM employee. A month before the Karnataka elections, the page's ownership in the registry was updated and transferred to an ABM administrator account with the email webprops@abmindia.org and the phone number of Mukul Jindal, a software engineer and a former ABM employee. A day after the *BoomLive* story was published, the registry was changed again to conceal the digital trail leading back to ABM.

Mehra and Jindal denied any connection with the website when *HuffPost India* contacted them.

In addition, *HuffPost India* stated that "ABM runs at least seven other popular pages for the BJP: Bharat Ke Mann Ki Baat (300k likes), Nation With NaMo (1.1 million likes), Phir Ek Baar Modi Sarkar (2.7 million likes), Mahathugbandhan (480k likes), India Unravelled (152k likes), My First Vote For Modi (74k likes) and Modi11…"

It added:

Nation With NaMo, the anchor for many of ABM's online activities, has posted at least four heavily edited videos that misrepresent opposition leader and Congress president Rahul Gandhi's statements on the tragic killing of at least 40 Indian troopers in Pulwama, Kashmir, on 14 February, and on loan waivers to indebted farmers. While the misleading clip on Pulwama garnered over 21,000 likes and 13,000 shares, the false video on loan waivers was shared over 67,000 times. Posts on ABM-managed sites, a current employee told *HuffPost India*, are optimised for virality. 'The more outrageous a post the better,' the ABM employee said. 'This is why they spread poison on Facebook'.

The *HuffPost India* story stated that ABM-managed Facebook pages go to great lengths to conceal their connections to India's ruling party. In December 2018, Facebook had said all accounts that place political advertisements must display a verified postal address and a valid phone number as part of the company's election transparency initiatives. For three ABM-managed Facebook pages – Nation With NaMo, Bharat Ke Mann Ki Baat and My First Vote For Modi – the only indication of their connection to the BJP is their listed postal address, which maps to the BJP headquarters in Delhi.

This dissimulation – incorrect contact details, out-of-service phone numbers – appear to go against Facebook's political advertisement transparency initiatives. Facebook has said the new rules are meant to give "people more information about who's responsible for the ads they see".

As part of the initiative, Facebook requires mandatory verification of physical postal addresses provided by political advertisers on its site – it doesn't always work.

When a *HuffPost India* reporter registered himself as a political advertiser, Facebook's third party verifier OnGrid simply texted the reporter saying he was verified. "If someone calls you," OnGrid's verifier texted, "Just say you were verified in person. Otherwise your ID may be blocked."

The *HuffPost India* article says that while the Association of Billion Minds has been "intimately involved" in the BJP's election plans, "it finds no mention in the party's campaign expenditure statements filed before the Election Commission of India." It added: "For example, ABM worked with MangoData, which describes itself as 'India's First AI (Artificial Intelligence) based adtech company,' to place political ads on Facebook..." MangoData did not respond to a request for comment.

The article went on to delineate a short history of the "Nation with NaMo" Facebook page that offers a glimpse into political consulting in India and the use of the social media to promote Modi, Amit Shah and the BJP.

19

Modi's App Spreads Falsehoods

Samarth Bansal wrote a detailed report on *DisFact*, an online newsletter (that was republished by *HuffPost India* on 27 January 2019) on the application named after India's Prime Minister. The report began with an account about a notorious post shared by one Sanjay Gupta in a Google Plus group named "Narendra Damodar Das Modi" in which he claimed that of the 40,000 victims of rape in India in a decade, as many as 39,000 had been raped by a Muslim. He added: "Still, Congress and Rahul Gandhi say that Hindus are rapists and terrorists. Shame on Congress and Gandhi family!"

This example of "news" had been completely concocted by a person who is the moderator of a group that claims to have 2.6 million members. In May, after the results of Karnataka assembly elections were declared, Gupta claimed: "92 per cent of the Muslims voted in Karnataka elections, 86 per cent Christians voted, but just 58 per cent Hindus. 42 per cent Hindus didn't even vote." This was again a piece of disinformation aimed at polarising two religious communities. Significantly Samarth wrote:

What's common to dozens of posts Gupta circulates on the group every day is the source: the bulk of his content, including the examples listed above, was originally posted on the Narendra Modi App (NaMo App), by its registered users.

The NaMo App is the personal mobile application of the Prime Minister of India on which any user who signs in can share images, videos and website links. "The visible lack of content moderation leaves the App as vulnerable to communal propaganda and fake news as Facebook, WhatsApp and Twitter," Samarth wrote, adding:

> ... the NaMo App has another unique aspect: the promoted accounts on the app's news feed, called "My Network." The feed, like on every social media platform, allows users to see all posts from people they follow in one place. But this section also promotes posts from a set of accounts. While these accounts share regular political updates on the prime minister's App, their Facebook pages openly circulate fake news... The promotion of such accounts on the NaMo App makes its millions of users vulnerable to misleading information.

> In an email response, Amit Malviya, head of BJP's IT cell, acknowledged that there is "some scope for misinformation" on the platform and "multiple posts have been taken down".

Launched in June 2015, ostensibly to enable ordinary citizens to connect with the Prime Minister and receive information about his government's policies and programmes, it had over ten million downloads at the time of writing. Malviya told Samarth that in November 2018, the NaMo App had an average of 1.43 million daily active users. The App was pre-installed in low-priced Reliance Jio smartphones that were distributed free by the BJP government in Chhattisgarh government before it lost the assembly elections.

On 14 November 2018, Jawaharlal Nehru's birth anniversary, Vijeta Malik, a state executive member of the BJP Haryana and the fifth most active user of the NaMo App, posted a fake quote attributed to Nehru saying he was "Christian by education, Muslim by culture and Hindu merely by accident" – a claim made by a critic of India's first Prime Minister. This person also distributed the fake quote supposedly made by Sachin Pilot (about helping Pakistan repay its debt instead of building a statue of Vallabhbhai Patel) mentioned earlier. Malik has made many other hateful posts against Muslims. Writes Samarth:

I found numerous posts shared from the NaMo App to other platforms (Facebook, WhatsApp, ShareChat, Google Plus) that make dubious claims, mostly coloured with a religious slant.

Spotting content shared through the NaMo App is simple: the posts shared through the App are auto-populated with "via MyNt" or "via NaMo App" phrase. It is usual for publishers to use the 'via' parameter for source attribution. For example, a news article shared from *The Indian Express* website on Twitter is appended with "via @IndianExpress."

One post shared from the NaMo App describes a meeting between Rahul Gandhi and Muslim intellectuals where Gandhi pledged never to wear a "'Janeu" (a sacred thread worn by Hindus) again. No such meeting ever took place.

Then there is an image of Congress headquarters that shows Rahul Gandhi signing a document in presence of other party leaders. In the backdrop is a framed portrait of Babur, the first emperor of the Mughal dynasty. "The image of Babur behind Rahul in the Congress headquarters is clearly telling the story of Muslim appeasement." The image, however, has been photoshopped to replace a framed photograph of Mahatma Gandhi's with Babur's portrait.

Malviya acknowledged somewhat reluctantly to Samarth over email:

My Network on the NaMo App allows volunteers, *karyakartas* and fans to freely express their feedback, views and opinion on various issues. When such a large volume of content is posted freely by volunteers, *karyakartas* and fans, there remains some scope for misinformation... Be it any platform or even the comments section of a news website, every platform where content is not editorialised faces this risk. Any post which is reported, is evaluated and treated according to our policies. Multiple posts have been taken down from time to time for various reasons. Everything ranging from content posting to content moderation is managed by volunteers... (and) gives a tailored experience to users based on geography, interests and popularity of content. To provide this experience, accounts of BJP leaders and popular user accounts are displayed to people in the corresponding region and interest group.

The "My Network" section of the App functions like a news feed, showing updates from users one follows on the NaMo App. Samarth wrote: "Some accounts are promoted: content from these accounts automatically appear in a user's news feed even if they have not followed those accounts, like a default feed. Users don't have an option to unfollow them," adding that most of the accounts promoted were those of Modi and BJP ministers like Prakash Javadekar, Ravi Shankar Prasad and Smriti Irani, among others.

The Facebook page of "The India Eye," which has 1.9 million followers, regularly shares disinformation. *AltNews* has established links between the page and Silver Touch Technologies Limited, the firm that built the NaMo App. Even as Himanshu Jain, the company's director, played innocent, his company had registered the domain name 'theindiaeye.in' and the website is hosted on the company's servers. *NDTV* reviewed documents that indicated that over half the business done by Silver Touch in 2016–17 worth around ₹62.5 crore came from government contracts.

Another account titled "Modi Bharosa" (or "Trust Modi") in the default news feed of the NaMo App, falsely claimed that Congress Rahul Gandhi ate meat during his journey to Mount Kailash alleging that he "respects traditions of Islam but insults Hinduism." The website was registered and managed in 2013–14 by a person who has been mentioned earlier in this book, namely, Anuj Gupta, who is now Officer on Special Duty (OSD) to Union Minister for Railways Piyush Goyal. Zankrut Oza, the other founder of the website reportedly led the "communications team" of Goyal and his ministry.

20

Fighting Fake News

Facebook's attempts at refurbishing its image and overcoming the crisis of credibility it is engulfed in, makes it reach out to critics from time and time and often co-opt them. As mentioned already, many media organisations in India are reluctant to criticise Facebook because they are recipients of financial support in the form of advertisements, sponsorship of events, and – ironically, but not surprisingly – training programmes and workshops aimed at "sensitising" users about the dangers of disinformation and fake news. On some occasions, these attempts at public relations and projecting the image of a good corporate citizen have met with a mixed response.

On 27 February 2019, Facebook organised an "external oversight workshop" to which over 20 "experts" were invited to participate. While their travel and accommodation was taken care of, the participants were asked to sign a "mutual non-disclosure agreement" committing them not to disclose what was going to be discussed during the closed-door sessions. We learnt that at least three so-called external experts who were invited, chose not to attend the workshop as they were uncomfortable signing the non-disclosure agreement.

The problem of tackling fake news has had an unexpected benefit, especially at a time when joblessness among the youth is a huge problem in India. On 16 March 2019, *Business Standard* reported that over 13,000 new jobs had been created for fact-checkers and news reviewers, including around 7,500 by Facebook alone. These persons were conversant in 15 Indian languages. At the same time, it was pointed out that most of these jobs were not permanent and contractual in nature.

There were other "positive" stories as well, albeit of a very different nature. In March 2018, in villages around Gadwal in Telangana, dozens of fake videos were circulated over WhatsApp. A particularly gory video depicted a man being disembowelled and claims were made in Telugu about a gang that was at large who were trying to harvest human organs and kidnapping children. Thanks to an alert policewoman Rema Rajeshwari, the rumours were scotched. She mobilised her staff and urged local residents to form cultural groups that travelled to villages singing songs and performing skits to raise awareness about the dangers of fake news.

Such stories are few and far between. That fake news is a major social problem in India is a no-brainer. A survey by Microsoft said 64 per cent of Indians had encountered fake news against a global average of 57 per cent.

Meanwhile, a start-up that began at the Indian Institute of Management Bangalore, developed an application for mobile phones named Litmus to detect fake news where those users who were successful in spotting fake news would get reward points – even the detection of misinformation and disinformation had become a game of sorts in the manner in which social media monopolies converted politics into games and contests.

★ ★ ★

In April 2018, Facebook stated in a media statement: "We have learned that once a story is rated as false, we have been able to reduce its distribution by 80 per cent, and thereby improve accuracy of information on Facebook and reduce misinformation."

Deposing before the US Congress, Mark Zuckerberg claimed his company would do everything it could to protect the integrity of elections in India and elsewhere. But if the situation in India is to be looked at, Facebook has a very long way to go to fulfill his stated intentions. Given the end-to-end encryption, which is supposed to be the unique feature of WhatsApp, posts on Facebook are far easier to track and take-down. Facebook allows advertisers to target users at a micro level. It also ensures that users stay in "echo chambers" reinforcing a "confirmation bias" – in other words, do not want to listen to views that are different from theirs and stay ideologically biased.

Initially, Facebook's dashboard could not be used to report non-English content at a time when more and more users of the platform were not using the English language. But that has since been refined and improved.

Facebook engaged the services of Mumbai-based *BoomLive* to counter fake news. However, Jency Jacob of *BoomLive* told *HuffPost India* that it did not receive much help from Facebook and used its own methods that were often painstaking to track misinformation, including "a combination of old school journalistic practices, such as getting fact-checkers to call sources, and tech tools like video and image matching software." Initially, fact-checks "could only be done on links and not on image, video, or text posts" but Facebook eventually granted *BoomLive* "access to image and video posts, but text posts are still beyond the purview of fact-checkers."

A *HuffPost India* article observed:

> For all its flaws, the fact-checking initiative appears to be making an attempt at solving the problem of misinformation on Facebook's news feed. But the company hasn't even begun to address the 800-pound gorilla that is WhatsApp. While Facebook has been castigated for playing fast and loose with privacy on its primary platform, the inherently better privacy features of the fully-encrypted Whatsapp platform have made it lethal when it comes to fake news... Unlike fake news that emerges on Facebook and Twitter, it is impossible to trace the source of misinformation on Whatsapp.

HuffPost argued that Facebook took "an easy route to find its Indian partners" – they are signatories of the prestigious Poynter Institute's International Fact Checking Network (IFCN), namely, *Factly*, *FactCrescendo*, *NewsMobile*, *TV Today Network Fact Check* (India Today Group), and *Vishvas News* (part of Jagran Media Network) besides a former signatory *BoomLive* and the international news agency *Agence France-*

Presse (AFP). Baybars Orsek, director, IFCN, told *HuffPost* in an emailed response:

> ...all signatories have to agree to abide by certain promises, beginning with a commitment to nonpartisanship and fairness. This means not just fact-checking news from across the political spectrum using the same methods, but also not concentrating their fact-checking on one side. Other commitments include being transparent about sources and methodology, and an open and honest corrections policy.

Currently, fact-checks are being carried out in six languages: English, Hindi, Bengali, Telugu, Malayalam, and Marathi. IFCN's Orsek noted that the organisation relies on assessors who verify all the requirements. The assessors are "expected and encouraged to take all editorial work of applicant organizations into account for their assessments and those assessments are taken very seriously by our advisory board, which consists of leaders in the fact-checking community and the decision whether to vet the applicant or not is taken on that board voting process," he said.

HuffPost India wrote:

> Orsek would not give details on how many Indian organisations had applied to become fact-checkers, or how many applications had been rejected, as the IFCN does not share that information. The network of assessors has to process all the information received, and works in local languages so that non-English fact-checkers can be audited. For each assessment that they conduct, the assessors are paid $350 (roughly ₹24,000). IFCN works with 86 external assessors,

who act as local experts. Of these, nine are in Asia, and just two in India, both teachers at the Indian Institute of Journalism and New Media in Bengaluru.

The website remained sceptical about the criteria used by IFCN to select fact-checking entities in India as well as the efficacy of the exercise. *HuffPost India* quoted an article published in the UK-based *Guardian* in which journalists working as fact-checkers with Facebook recounted their "frustrations" with Facebook. "They've essentially used us for crisis PR," Brooke Binkowski, former managing editor of fact-checking website Snopes, reportedly remarked, adding: "They're not taking anything seriously. They are more interested in making themselves look good and passing the buck... They clearly don't care."

Facebook disputed these views but the BBC reported that the *Associated Press* (*AP*) news agency and Snopes had "stopped their work with the company."

Conclusion

Facebook founder Mark Zuckerberg wrote in an op-ed article in *The Washington Post* on 30 March: "I believe we need a more active role for governments and regulators..." in regulating the internet. He added: "By updating the rules for the internet, we can preserve what's best about it – the freedom to express themselves and for entrepreneurs to build new things – while also protecting society from broader harms."

He argued that new regulations are needed in four areas: harmful content, protection of the democratic rights of citizens, particularly during elections, ensuring user privacy (along the lines proposed by the European Union.

After opposing and resisting government intervention, Zuckerberg appeared to have changed track when he urged governments of more countries to adopt measures to protect the privacy of users and curb the abuse of social media platforms. There was widespread condemnation when, on 15 March, 28-year-old white supremacist Brenton Harrison Tarrant opened fire killing 50 Muslims who were praying at two mosques in Christchurch, New Zealand, and broadcast a part of the gruesome massacre live on Facebook.

The governments of Australia and New Zealand are mulling restrictions on social media that include prior permission before live-streaming, delayed online broadcasts, vetting of content and even prison terms for executives of companies who fail to censor violence and hate. Australia's Prime Minister Scott Morrison said on 30 March: "Big social media companies have a responsibility to take every possible action to ensure their technology products are not exploited by murderous terrorists... It should not just be a matter of doing the right thing. It should be the law... It is impossible to remove all harmful content from the internet but when people use dozens of different sharing services – all with their own policies and processes – we need a more standardized approach."

As Damien Cave of *The New York Times* wrote:

> The push for government intervention... reflects a surge of anger in countries more open to restrictions on speech than in the US, and growing impatience with digital companies seen as more worried about their business models than local concerns. There are precedents for the kinds of regulation under consideration. At one end of the spectrum is China, where the world's most sophisticated system of internet censorship stifles almost all political debate along with hate speech and pornography – but without preventing the rise of homegrown companies (like those in the Alibaba group) making sizable profits. No one in Australia or New Zealand is suggesting that this should be the model. But the other end of the spectrum – the 24/7 bazaar of instant user-generated content – also looks increasingly unacceptable to people in this part of the world...

How can a middle ground be found between the two ends of the spectrum? How can national concerns be dovetailed into what drives a profit-maximising global conglomerate? As Jacinda Ardern, New Zealand's Prime Minister – who earned kudos for her sensitively handling of the situation after Tarrant's killing spree – pointed out: "Ultimately we can all promote good rules locally but these platforms are global."

Many unanswered questions remain. Can an international consensus emerge on how to regulate the chaotic world of online social networks? Should the internet be treated as a public utility and governed accordingly? If indeed there is a movement towards arriving at a worldwide agreement on internet governance, who should be among the important stakeholders: representatives of governments of nation-states, United Nations organisations and other multilateral bodies, the digital monopolies, persons who are well-versed in technology, scholars from the world of academics, besides representatives of civil society?

Even if all stakeholders participate in the consensus-building process, the weights and representation granted to each of the sections would remain a point of contention that would not be resolved easily. Be that as it may, there is at present growing agreement among all stakeholder groups that Facebook is reacting because it is under intense attack. Critics of the organisation say that the social media giant knew for a long time that its policies and enforcement mechanisms were far from adequate and largely ineffective.

Pratik Sinha of *AltNews* asserts that fake news should not be seen as an aberration but as a highly-organised, well-funded "industry" in India that ensures disinformation is disseminated in a "professional" manner to enhance "believability" and to arouse the emotions of users. He gave an example of the Facebook page called "Phir Ek Bar Modi Sarkar" ("The Modi government will return again") that puts out well-produced content. Sinha told us: "You can look at the graphics, the videos. It's not just some random dude sitting and producing this. There's a team which is doing this."

The problem he and others flag is that big bucks are going into the fake news "industry." Political parties will not disclose the amounts that are being covertly spent while bodies like the Election Commission of India will not be able to ascertain the amounts that are being poured into "surrogate" Facebook pages and websites for campaigning and political propaganda by proxies and "volunteers." Despite claims to the contrary, Facebook's activities remain highly non-transparent and the situation is unlikely to change in a hurry. Sinha asks: "Do citizens not deserve to know where this money is coming from and who are the individuals behind this propaganda?"

The founder of *AltNews* points out that it is important to understand the socio-economic profiles of typical users of Facebook and WhatsApp in India. The former tend to belong to a relatively higher social and economic group. On the other hand, WhatsApp is being increasingly used by users cutting across the country's class and caste divisions. In fact, it is argued that for many in the lower socio-segments of the population, WhatsApp is the "preferred" platform of communication and for receiving information.

Sinha says the well-organised and well-funded nature of the disinformation "industry" in the country allows it to react very quickly to information considered newsworthy or topical.

He provides the example of Gurmehar Kaur who put out a video with her holding slides to puncture the jingoistic claims that were being made. In no time at all, a fake video of a young woman apparently drinking and dancing on top of a car was circulated with the aim of tarnishing Kaur's reputation among conservative sections of Indian society.

Many in the country are vulnerable to extreme emotional reactions, especially when it comes to religious sentiments. Purveyors of disinformation have been particularly adept in creating a toxic atmosphere in India. What then is the way forward? One important task is to raise awareness. What is also important is that social media users start questioning more, become sceptical and not become excessively dependent on receiving information from one, or a few, sources so that they can get a well-rounded perspective of issues.

There is more than enough technical expertise that is available in the public domain on ways of detecting photo-shopped images, morphed pictures, sliced audio recordings and spliced videos. However, many ordinary users of social media unfortunately do not have the time or the competence to delve deeper into detecting disinformation and falsehood. It is easier to passively and unquestioningly accept and believe what is provided to us. This attitude too needs changing. As our book has tried to show, disinformation not only distorts reality but can maim and murder as well. The sooner we realise this ugly aspect of the new digital world around us the better.

Annexure: Safeguarding Democracy from Digital Platforms

Text of statement issued on 5 April 2019 as an outcome of collective reflection and a consultative process involving civil society organisations, including Common Cause, Constitutional Conduct, Internet Freedom Foundation, Free Software Movement of India, Association for Democratic Reforms and retired civil servants, including two former Chief Election Commissioners N Gopalaswami and S Y Quraishi.

Ahead of the 2019 Lok Sabha elections, the role of digital platforms, such as Google, Facebook and Twitter, and the threat India's democracy faces from these platforms, have to be scrutinised closely. It has been estimated that Google and Facebook control nearly 70 per cent of global internet traffic. From India to Brazil, we see WhatsApp, owned by Facebook, becoming the most important means of communication for many, with over 200 million users in India alone.

It is also clear by now that these entities are no longer mere communication platforms but serve as media organizations as well. In western countries, ad spending on digital media has outstripped that on print and television. In India, too, there has been a drastic rise in the same.

The digital platforms today have the ability to influence

165

people's behaviour on an enormous scale, and, therefore, also the election process. Google and Facebook, as well as independent researchers, have analysed the impact of these platforms on influencing electoral processes and have concluded that there could be a significant swing in results through manipulation of electoral news feeds.

The impact of the rise of these digital monopolies on the democratic process was partially revealed with the Cambridge Analytica scandal. Cambridge Analytica, using data from Facebook, is believed to have generated profiles on millions of users which were reportedly used by campaigns in the US elections for targeted messaging. In Brazil, during the presidential elections, allegations surfaced about business interests close to the far-right candidate and eventual winner, Jair Bolsonaro, illegally using WhatsApp to send millions of defamatory messages trashing his main rival.

The 2014 election campaign gave us the first hints of the kind of influence digital platforms could have on popular perception. The campaign of the BJP, led by Narendra Modi, is believed to have spent substantial amounts for the campaign, a sizeable part of it being spent on media advertising alone. Today, with a far higher number of voters on digital platforms such as Facebook, YouTube, WhatsApp, and a host of other platforms, the influence of digital platforms on the elections will obviously be greater than in the preceding ones.

Taking the cue from the BJP's campaign, many political parties have set up IT Cells, contracting IT professionals and political consultancy firms to crunch data and launch fine-tuned campaigns targeted at specific demographics, mainly through Facebook and Twitter. All of this could be outside of

EC regulations, lacking in transparency or regulatory control of ECI unless effective steps are taken. Recent media reports have revealed the extent of cooperation between Facebook and the BJP campaign, including key personnel who worked in both.

The apps of various parties, which are reported to be gathering a lot of information for profiling and targeting, need to be monitored and brought under the regulatory oversight of the Election Commission.

India has a fairly robust electoral code of conduct, which scrutinizes campaigning on the ground and through conventional media, but the same has not translated to a scrutiny of online campaigning. This has enabled the political parties, which could mobilise large amounts of money – the BJP being way ahead of the pack – to spend substantially on digital media without any checks and balances.

In the years since 2014, the number of smartphone users has doubled, and the number of WhatsApp users has increased more than five-fold. In the various elections since 2014, we have seen the use of WhatsApp to spread communally charged and polarising messages and fake news on a massive scale. This election is likely to be no different.

Parties with the capacity to spend may even use, for example, WhatsApp Business Application Program Interfaces to deliver messages to very specific demographics, further dividing the electorate, and marking yet another milestone in the misuse of data collected by digital giants.

Unlike campaigning through other forms of media, digital media campaigns are often difficult to analyse as both the amount of money involved and the methodology used for targeting remains in the background, and are the exclusive domain of the digital monopolies. Similarly, unlike other media, there are few regulations across the globe on campaigns through digital media.

On a positive note, in the aftermath of the Cambridge Analytica scandal, there have been attempts by both digital monopolies and governments to document and regulate ad spending. Recently, Facebook has announced the 'paid for' and 'published by' features for all political ads, as well as a publicly accessible library which will archive these ads. Google has announced similar measures, while Twitter has said all political ad spending will be visible on a dashboard. However, these steps are not enough considering the scale of the upcoming elections in India. A much more broad-based campaign, involving multiple stakeholders – political parties, civil society and the Election Commission – is necessary to ensure that these platforms are not used to determine electoral results.

We note that the Election Commission's consultations with digital platforms and the Internet and Mobile Association of India (IAMAI) have culminated in the adoption of a Voluntary Code of Ethics effective from March 20, 2019. We understand that the digital platforms have committed to bringing about a certain measure of transparency in respect of political ads, instituting a mechanism for handling complaints of misuse, and enforcing the 48 hour silence before the end of poll on social media. While we welcome this outcome as a step forward, it needs to be pointed out that the Code has been drafted without any transparency, public inputs or civil society engagement. The participation of all key stakeholders is of crucial importance in a consultation of this nature. We also note that the Code is not binding, has no legal force, and does not address the larger issues that we have articulated in this note.

In this respect, certain suggestions are being made to uphold and defend the integrity of the next general elections.

Appeal to the Political Parties:

It is critical for our electoral process and the health of our democracy that the role of money power in elections should be restricted. For last two decades, a proposal to limit the expenditure of political parties in elections has not been acted upon by any government. We appeal to all political parties to recognise the threat of money power in the elections and evolve a consensus to enact a legislation to cap the expenditure of political parties in elections. Since the parties are now preparing their manifestos, we urge them to include therein a firm commitment to work for such a cap in future elections.

Appeal to the Election Commission

1. *Monitor compliance*: The Election Commission of India should monitor the online spending of political parties for election campaigns, and not just spending by candidates.

2. *Disclosure by Political Parties on their IT Cells, contractors and ads to the ECI*: Make it mandatory for political parties to disclose official Political Party/Individual handles on all major platforms such as Facebook, Twitter as well as lesser known platforms such as WeChat, Sharechat, TikTok, etc.

a) The EC must direct all political parties to disclose the names of companies and paid consultants looking after their social media, IT cell, digital marketing, as well as nodal digital officers.

b) Political parties must submit details of all digital spending during the election campaign process. These details must be made public.

c) The Election Commission must direct candidates to disclose their social media handles and campaign spends. Also ask to provide information on paid consultants posting on their behalf or otherwise officially promoting them. All "Office of (Candidate name)" social media accounts involved in campaigning or in coordination of communications in relation to electoral matters, must also be listed.

d) The EC must direct candidates and political parties to provide information on all contracts signed by them with third party vendors for digital services and disclose this publicly.

Improve transparency:

Recently, digital platforms have announced steps for greater transparency on digital spending. Some of these measures include declaration of the identity of those paying for/ publishing ads, as well as various kinds of verification. It is important in this context that there be a common understanding of what constitutes a political ad. The Election Commission must initiate a process involving political parties and tech firms which evolves common definitions on such ads. Similarly, the verification process announced by various firms must be certified by the Election Commission and must be transparent. These safeguards have been implemented in other countries, too, especially the US, but reports have pointed to the ease with which they can be bypassed. The Election Commission must conduct an independent audit of the declaration processes for political ads. Specific steps may include:

a) Direct digital platforms to aggregate and provide it details regarding electoral ad/promotion spend, as well as information on expenditures for ads/promotions by political parties and their listed IT cells and social media promoters. This information must be made public.

b) Direct digital platforms to track the monetisation of posts (the practice of paying money to boost the visibility of posts) on social media platforms by political parties, as well as by individuals representing these parties. The digital platforms should also disclose the specific demographics being targeted. The amounts spent on monetised posts and the identities of their target groups should be made public.

c) Caution all major internet and social media firms that foreign funded, advertisements supporting or assisting political candidates entail a violation of Indian laws, including the Foreign Contributions (Regulation) Act.

d) Request relevant governments/departments in the US, UK, and the EU for any filings/data pertaining to services, compensation offered to candidates running for office required to be filed under the foreign bribery laws of such countries (for example, the US Foreign Corrupt Practices Act, UK Anti-Bribery Act).

Build institutional capacity:

The Election Commission must create a nodal department to address the growing threat of fake news which has the potential to jeopardise free and fair elections in the country. Headed by a competent and senior officer and staffed by members with the requisite technical capabilities, the department can also receive complaints and grievances from the public, candidates, or political parties.

Prevent profiling and hate speech:

The Election Commission should ensure that Facebook and digital platforms should not be used to target communities on the lines of caste, religion, ethnicity and linguistic identity, or in any other way that violates the electoral code of conduct. The same regulations should be applicable for apps developed by/for political parties.

a) Digital platforms must not do anything that influences the voting process in anyway.

b) All digital firms must establish a robust and transparent complaints mechanism, with nodal officers to deal with reports of violations of norms on their platforms.

c) Digital platforms must conduct outreach programmes to their users to familiarize them with the process of complaints. Digital firms should also make public the process by which they deal with these complaints so as to enable audit of the corrective measures.

Additional steps to strengthen the environment for free and fair elections:

a) The Election Commission should reveal any discussions it

has had with digital giants in the run–up to the elections about the process.

b) The Elections Commission should conduct an outreach programme, educating social media users on ways to report violations of electoral norms.

Some specific steps include:

i. Engage with news organisations, civil society, and other independent groups seeking to combat disinformation, hate news circulation, and improve fact-checking during the poll process

ii. Set up mechanisms to collaborate with the independent civil society, new media groups and political parties in order to focus on fact-checking.

iii. Call for an open, consultative meeting with experts and independent actors working on electoral integrity and combating disinformation, besides discussions with web firms, government departments, and political parties.

iv. Require all party digital/IT leads to be informed of the current MCC media guidelines, social media guidelines, and Indian Penal Code provisions.

v. Put in place curbs on data brokers which are in the business of collecting large volumes of data and selling it to political parties. There are reports of many such agencies already having conducted vast data collection exercises ahead of the elections. The EC should insist that political parties report any such transactions.

vi. Ensure that any voter id collected as part of any

initiative by other government agencies should be immediately deleted from the latter's database so that it is not used for electoral purposes.

Acknowledgements

This work would not have been possible without the support of my sister and my friends. Thank you, guys. I also want to thank everyone who put themselves in danger and spoke to us for this work.

– Cyril Sam

The writing of this book would have been impossible but for the support of many individuals, several of whom chose anonymity. One gave up a lucrative corporate career to become a political activist while another sought to atone for his past "sins" – namely, providing unstinted support to Narendra Modi and believing his tall claim that *achhe din* (good times) would soon come to the country. Two other journalists gave us invaluable help with translating the English text for the Hindi version of the book and suggested ways in which we could reach out to a wider audience. A number of persons who chose to remain unnamed gave us valuable information and insights.

Acknowledgements

Among those who can be named, I am especially indebted to Prabir Purkayastha who has for long been unequivocally opposed to digital monopolies like Facebook and WhatsApp and who provided me a most conducive "dungeon" to work out of in the office of *NewsClick*. My dear friend, Professor Pradip Kumar ("PK") Datta and Shankar Raghuraman sustained me with their constructive criticism and constant questioning.

I am thankful to Subir Ghosh who put together the website with financial support from the National Foundation for India. Those who helped him were researchers Pallavi Krishnappa and Tatsita Mishra.

Manish Purohit of AuthorsUpFront, my publishing associate over the last five years, took care of the logistics and administrative work that goes into the thankless aspects of producing and distributing the book. The book's cover was designed by Shamik Kundu of PealiDezine, Ram Das Lal typeset the manuscript and the promotional videos put together by Sukanya Datta Majumdar and Saurabh Paul.

I am particularly grateful to Cyril Sam, the lead author of the book who kept asking me very difficult questions about how we were working while gathering information and why we were writing what we did – and to Wenceslaus Mendes for introducing Cyril to me.

I am greatly indebted to my family: Jaya, Triveni, Purnajyoti, Narendra (Nana-ji) Bhatnagar, Tapati, Hari and Mrinalini. The lonely and tedious aspects of writing were compensated for by their affection. My parents Krishna and Pranab, and my mother-in-law Shakuntala, are no more physically present with us but I felt their presence as I wrote and edited the manuscript.

– **Paranjoy Guha Thakurta**

About the Authors

Cyril Sam is a freelance journalist and researcher based out of New Delhi. His interests lie at the intersection of technology and the business of news media. In the past, he has been associated with the *International Center for Journalists, Scroll.in, Catch News, Tehelka* and *Firstpost*.

Paranjoy Guha Thakurta is a journalist and author with work experience spanning more than four decades, cutting across different media: print, radio, television and documentary cinema. He is a writer, speaker, anchor, interviewer, teacher and commentator in English, Bengali and Hindi. He served as editor of the *Economic and Political Weekly* between April 2016 and July 2017. He is currently a consultant with *NewsClick*. He is also an author or a co-author of books including *Loose Pages: Court Cases that could have Shaken India – Recalling the Birla-Sahara Papers and Kalikho Pul's Suicide Note, Gas Wars: Crony Capitalism and the Ambanis, Thin Dividing Line: India, Mauritius and Global Illicit Financial Flows, Sue The Messenger: How Legal Harassment by Corporates Shackles Reportage and*

Undermines Democracy in India, Media Ethics: Truth, Fairness and Objectivity and *Divided We Stand: India in a Time of Coalitions.* He is a publisher of books and has produced and directed a number of documentary films. He teaches courses on the media at various educational institutions, including three Indian Institutes of Management. He is on the boards of several civil society organisations. He participates frequently in, and organizes, seminars and conferences. He is a regular contributor to publications and websites and frequently appears on the radio and television channels as an anchor as well as analyst. Details about his work can be accessed at www.paranjoy.in.

Index

179

Index

Index

Index

Index

Index